Selected Ancient Chinese Royal Recipes

Chief-Editor: Song Nong
Translator: Li Guohua,   Zhao Wentao

Academy Press [Xue Yuan]

First Edition 1997
ISBN7 - 5077 - 1290 - 7

Selected Ancient Chinese Royal Recipes
Chief - Editor: Song Nong
Translator: Li Guohua,   Zhao Wentao

Published by
Academy Press [Xue Yuan]
11 Wanshoulu Xijie, Beijing 100036, China

Distributed by
China International Book Trading Corporation
35 Chegongzhuang Xilu, Beijing 100044, China
P. O. Box 399, Beijing, China

Printed in the People's Republic of China

Preface

Traditional Chinese Medicine and Pharmacology (TCMP) has a long history. It summed up abundant clinical experience in the struggle against diseases. It has formed an integrated, unique and first of all, a scientific system of both theory and clinical practice. On the fundamental principle of 'Zhengtiguannian' (Wholism) and 'Bianzhenglunzhi' (Treatment of the same disease with different therapies). TCM treatment is effective for various kinds of diseases with few side-effect taken. At present, a great upsurge in learning, practising and studying TCM is just in the ascendant. For the benefit of people of all countries, we compiled this series of 'Collections of Traditional Chinese Medicine' in order to promote the spread of TCM all over the world.

In this book, we introduced comprehensively Selected Ancient Chinese Royal Recipes. This book is the best for those foreign friends who are interested in learning traditional Chinese medicine.

May everyone of all nations enjoy a healthy life!

Chief - Editor

Contents

Chapter One   Internal Diseases ······························· (1)
    SECTION   1   Common Cold ························ (1)
    SECTION   2   Cough ································· (9)
    SECTION   3   Chronic Bronchitis ················ (17)
    SECTION   4   Bronchial Asthma ················· (24)
    SECTION   5   Pulmonary Tuberculosis ········· (33)
    SECTION   6   Chronic Gastritis ················· (38)
    SECTION   7   Peptic Ulcer ······················· (43)
    SECTION   8   Hepatitis ··························· (48)
    SECTION   9   Constipation ······················· (58)
    SECTION 10   Malaria ···························· (66)
    SECTION 11   Hematochezia ···················· (69)
    SECTION 12   Ascites ····························· (71)
    SECTION 13   Hypertension ······················ (73)
    SECTION 14   Coronary Heart Disease ········· (93)
    SECTION 15   Hyperthyroidism ················· (104)
    SECTION 16   Simple Obesity ··················· (107)
    SECTION 17   Insolation ························ (109)
    SECTION 18   Simple Goiter ···················· (112)
    SECTION 19   Urinary Infection ················ (115)
    SECTION 20   Stone of Urinary System ······ (117)

SECTION 21	Nephritis	(120)
SECTION 22	Impotency	(124)
SECTION 23	Chronic Prostatitis	(127)
SECTION 24	Hyperplasia of Prostate	(132)
SECTION 25	Headache	(139)
SECTION 26	Dizziness	(144)
SECTION 27	Insomnia	(147)
SECTION 28	Diabetes	(150)

Chapter Two Surgical Diseases ······ (161)

SECTION 1	Furuncle, carbuncle, and cellulitis	(161)
SECTION 2	Scrofula	(163)
SECTION 3	Acute Mastitis	(165)
SECTION 4	Hernia	(168)
SECTION 5	Hemorrhoids	(170)
SECTION 6	Prolapse of Rectum	(172)
SECTION 7	Angiitis	(174)

Chapter Three Gynecological and Obstetrical Diseases ······ (177)

SECTION 1	Dysmenorrhea	(177)
SECTION 2	Amenorrhea	(182)
SECTION 3	Irregular Menstruation	(184)
SECTION 4	Climacteric Syndrome	(189)
SECTION 5	Prolapse of Uterus	(192)

SECTION 6	Dysfunctional Uterine Bleeding	(195)
SECTION 7	Habitual Abortion	(199)
SECTION 8	Sterility	(203)
SECTION 9	Leukorrhagia	(206)
SECTION 10	Vomiting During Pregnancy	(209)
SECTION 11	Edema During Pregnancy	(213)
SECTION 12	Lack of Lactation	(215)
SECTION 13	Recipes for Delactation	(219)

Chapter Four　Pediatric Diseases ······ (221)

SECTION 1	Common Cold in Children	(221)
SECTION 2	Cough and Asthma in Children	(223)
SECTION 3	Wooping Cough	(225)
SECTION 4	Morbilli Measles	(227)
SECTION 5	Varicella	(230)
SECTION 6	Parotitis	(232)
SECTION 7	Anorexia	(235)
SECTION 8	Infantile Malnutrition	(239)
SECTION 9	Diarrhea in Children	(241)
SECTION 10	Retention of Food	(244)
SECTION 11	Enuresis	(246)
SECTION 12	Rachitis	(249)
SECTION 13	Nocturnal Fretfulness in Infants	(251)

SECTION 14	Infantile Polysialia	....	(253)
SECTION 15	Acute Nephritis in Children	...	(255)

Chapter Five Orthopedic and Traumatic Diseases .... (257)

SECTION	1	Osteomyelitis and Bone Tuberculosisi	(257)
SECTION	2	Fracture	(259)
SECTION	3	Traumata	(261)

Chapter Six Dermatoses .... (263)

SECTION	1	Urticaria	(263)
SECTION	2	Neurodermatitis	(266)
SECTION	3	Eczema	(269)
SECTION	4	Herpes Zoster	(272)
SECTION	5	Acne	(275)
SECTION	6	Miliaria (Prickly Heat)	(278)
SECTION	7	Chilblain	(280)

Chapter Seven Diseases of Eyes, Ears, Nose, and Throat .... (283)

SECTION	1	Acute Conjunctivitis	(283)
SECTION	2	Ulcerative Blepharitis	(286)
SECTION	3	Nyctalopia	(288)
SECTION	4	Glaucoma	(290)
SECTION	5	Chronic Rhinitis	(291)

SECTION 6	Acute and Chronic Nasosinusitis ······ (295)
SECTION 7	Epistaxis ······ (302)
SECTION 8	Acute Suppurative Otitis Media ······ (307)
SECTION 9	Acute and Chronic Pharyngitis ······ (313)
SECTION 10	Toothache ······ (320)
SECTION 11	Acute Tonsillitis ······ (323)

Chapter One Internal Diseases

SECTION 1 Common Cold

Common cold is one of the most common diseases, and is characterized by fever, aversion to cold, nasal obstruction, runny nose, sneezing, coughing and headache. This disease can occur in all four seasons, but more commonly in winter and spring when there is a drastic change in weather, and in cases of all ages. The younger the patients are, the more the complications there will be. This is the principal characteristic of the common cold of children, which does not appear in adults.

ETIOLOGY AND PATHOGENESIS

Pathogenic wind is the predominant etiological factor in colds. It invades the upper respiratory tract and the body surface when body resistance is low, which typically occurs when there is a sudden climatic change. The pathogenic wind combines with cold in winter, heat in spring and damp − heat in summer, taking advantage of untimely climatic changes to attack the body.

The attack on the body is closely related to body resistance, so if one's vital energy is low due to an irregular life style, drenching by rain, negligence regarding changes in temperature or overfatigue, the likelihood of invasion increases. A patient with chronic bronchitis or bronchiectasis is also vulnerable. Furthermore, the body's constitution plays a role in the affection. A person with a yang deficiency is susceptible to wind − cold, and one with a yin deficiency is susceptible to wind − heat.

Because pathogenic wind invades through the upper respiratory tract and the body surface, pathological changes are confined to these portions of the body. When pathogenic factors obstruct the upper respiratory tract, respiratory symptoms occur, such as cough and stuffy nose. The confrontation between the body's resistance and pathogenic factors at the superficial portion of the body results in chilliness and fever.

In case of delicate visceral organs, thin skin and weak Wei − system in combination with sudden change of the weather, the six exopathogenic factors are apt to attack the superficies to cause failure of superficial qi, disorder of opening and closing function of skin striae and inhibition of yang energy, manifested by fever and chills, headache, running and stuffy nose, cough etc..

In young cases of common cold, fever may be severe. It is because young children are of pure yang bodies and the invasion of evils is liable to bring about heat. Because of the delicate lungs in young cases, when they are attacked by evils, the lung - qi will stagnate, and qi will be out of order, and the body fluids may accumulate to form sputum, obstructing the air passages, causing productive cough. The spleen of young cases is not fully developed. If their diet is not proper after being attacked, the digestive function may be involved, milk and food may stagnate in the middle - jiao. They may present with distention of gastric cavity and abdomen, poor appetite for milk and food, vomiting or diarrhea, and some other dyspeptic symptoms. The invasion of evils will cause heat and fire, affecting the spirit, leading to vigilance and restlessness, even infantile convulsion. This is known as cold with convulsion in pediatrics.

MAIN POINTS OF DIAGNOSIS

1. **Main Symptoms and Signs:** It is mostly manifested by sudden onset, fever with no or little sweat, running and stuffy nose, sore throat, mild cough, etc. The body temperature is varied with different strains of pathogen type of disease and individual condition. Infants and younger children

tend to have higher temperature than the older ones, sometimes reaching 40℃, but with better general condition. Older children have more severe localized symptoms of the nose, pharynx and throat.

2. **Complications:** In infants and young children, it is usually associated with high fever, convulsion or vomiting, diarrhea, abdominal pain, anorexia or productive cough, and even bronchitis or pneumonia.

3. Some acute infectious diseases such as measles, chicken pox, scarlet fever, epidemic mumps, epidemic encephalomyelitis, etc. have the same manifestations as colds in their early stages, but different features will soon be found later. So early identification is very necessary.

Recipe 1

Ingredients

litchi (*Fructus litchi*)   30 g

millet wine   right amount

Process   Decoct the litchi in millet wine over a slow fire.

Directions   Take it warmly.

Indications   Common cold due the deficiency of Qi.

Recipe 2

Ingredients

atractylodes rhizome (*Rhizoma Atractylodis*)

Chapter One

magnolia bark（*Cortex Magnoliae Officinalis*）
Chuanxiong Rhizome（*Rhizoma Ligustici Chuanxiong*）
bupleurum root（*Radix Bupleuri*）
agastache（*Herba Agastachis*）
pinellia tuber（*Rhizoma Pinelliae*）
dried orange peel（*Pericarpium Citri*）
liquorice（*Radix Glycyrrhizae*）

Process　Take them in equal portions, decoct them in right amount of water until it is nearly done.

Directions　Take it warmly, have a rest for perspiration.

Indications　Common cold.

Recipe 3

Ingredients

honeysuckle flower（*Flos Lonicerae*）	30 g
hawthorn fruit（*Fructus Crataegi*）	10 g
honey（*Mel*）	250 g

Process　Decoct the honeysuckle flower and hawthorn in water over a strong fire, when it have boil for $3-5$ minutes, sift out the decoction; add right amount of water in the dregs, then decoct it again and sift out the decoction, put all the decoction together and honey it with honey.

Directions　Take it warmly.

Indications　Common cold.

Recipe 4

Ingredients

> *bupleurum root* (*Radix Bupleuri*)   10 g
> *pinellia tuber* (*Rhizoma Pinelliae*)   6 g
> *Chinese - date* (*Fructus Ziziphi Jujubae*)
>   4.5 g
> *scutellaria root* (*Radix Scutellariae*)   3 g
> *cinnamon twig* (*Ramulus Cinnamomi*)   3 g
> *white peony root* (*Radix Paeoniae Alba*)   3 g
> *glehnia root* (*Radix Glehniae*)   2 g
> *ginger* (*Zingiberis*)   2 g
> *liquorice* (*Radix Glycyrrhizae*)   2 g

Process   Decoct them in water for two times, sift out the decoction and mix them well.

Directions   Take it three times a day.

Indications   Influenza.

Recipe 5

Ingredients

> *polished round - grained rice* (*Semen Oryzae Sativae*)   50 g
> *scallion stalks* (*Bulbus Allii Fistulosi*) *three sections and 3 cm for each section*
> *prepared soybean*   10 g
> *white sugar*   right amount

Process　Make the rice into gruel, when it is nearly done, add in the scallion section, prepared soya bean, go on cooking until it come to several boils, season it with sugar.

Directions　Take it warmly, two doses daily for 2 days successively.

Indications　Common cold of wind − cold.

Recipe 6

Ingredients

sesame thick sauce　　　　　　right amount
brown sugar　　　　　　　　　right amount
tea leaves (*Tea*) a few

Process　Mix the first two ingredients well and infuse it and tea with boiling water.

Directions　Take it warmly.

Indications　Common cold at attack stage.

Recipe 7

Ingredients

dried orange peel (*Pericarpium Citri*)　15 g
bupleurum root (*Radix Bupleuri*)　15 g
forsythia fruit (*Fructus Forsythiae*)　15 g
dahurian Angelica root (*Radix Angelicae Dahuricae*)　15 g
Immature bitter orange (*Fructus Aurantii Immaturus*)　15 g

Internal Diseases

  hawthorn fruit（*Fructus Crataegi*） 15 g
  notopterygium root（*Rhizoma seu Radix Notopterygii*） 15 g
  root of purple – flowered peucedanum（*Radix Peucedani*） 15 g
  ledebouriella root（*Radix Ledebouriellae*） 15 g
  agastache（*Herba Pogostemonis seu Agastachis*） 15 g
  liquorice（*Radix Glycyrrhizae*） 15 g
  medicated leaven（*Massa Fermentata Medicinalis*） 15 g
  Chuanxiong Rhizome（*Rhizoma Ligustici Chuanxiong*） 15 g
  magnolia bark（*Cortex Magnoliae Officinalis*） 15 g
  platycodon root（*Radix Platycodi*） 15 g
  germinated barley（*Fructus Hordei Germinatus*） 15 g
  perilla leaf（*Folium Perillae*） 15 g
  old tea leaves（*Tea*） 100 g

 Process Grind all them into fine powder.

 Directions Take 10 g of fine powder with hot water.

 Indications Common cold.

Chapter One

SECTION 2 Cough

Cough is a common disease, which occurs in all four seasons, especially in winter and spring. The incidence is high in babies under three years of age. The younger the cases are, the more severe the pathological conditions will be. Cough is often caused by invasion of external pathogenic factors, its duration short and its prognosis good.

When lung and defensive qi are weak, the external pathogenic wind − cold or wind − heat is likely to invade the lung system via the mouth, nose and skin pores, thus impairing the function of the lung in dispersing and descending. Subsequently, cough will result. Retention of phlegm − damp in the spleen and lung can also cause cough when induced by invasion of external pathogenic factors.

ETIOLOGY AND PATHOGENESIS

1. **Cough attacked by exogenous pathogenic factors.**

When weather is changeable in winter and spring, six exogenous pathogenic factors will easily attack the lung, resulting in cough due to impairment of purifying and descending function of the lung and abnormal rising of lung − qi. As the result of the sluggishness of lung − qi, the interior retention and accumulation of the body fluid will form sputum, obstructing the air passage and inducing productive cough.

2. **Stagnation of phlegm in the interior**. The stagnation of dampness may be transformed into sputum which will store in the lung, block the air passage and inhibit ventilation.

3. **Weak constitution**. People are apt to be invaded by exogenous pathogenic factors if they are congenitally deficient and weak in constitution. The invasion brings about recurrent cough. Chronic cough will injure the spleen and the lung and result in cough by the internal injury due to deficiency of both the spleen and the lung, and the consumption of the lung − yin.

MAIN POINTS OF DIAGNOSIS

1. The initial onset of the cough caused by exogenous pathogenic factors is mostly accompanied by cold symptoms such as chilliness, fever, stuffy nose with watery discharge, headache, general muscular pains, redness and itching of the throat. After one or two days, it is chiefly marked by cough.

Chapter One

At first, the cough may present with deep, loud or raucous sound, which is mild during the day and severe at night, associated with vomiting, and thin whitish or thick yellowish sputum. However, young children are unable to spit.

2. Cough caused by internal injury is commonly seen in the cases with delicate constitution and malnutrition. These people are likely to catch a cold and will be more severely attacked by pathogenic factors. The course of the disease is rather long, manifested by cough low cough with thin whitish or less thick sputum or associated with fever.

Recipe

Ingredients

Sichuan fritillary bulb (*Bulb Fritillariae Cirrhosae*)   5 g

soft-shelled turtle (*Trioyx Sinensis*)   1 (about 500 g)

soup of the chicken   1000 g

scallion, ginger, prickly ash peel, millet wine, salt   right amount for each

Process   Kill the soft-shell turtle, get rid of the head and entrails, cut it into cubes, put them in a bowl, add other ingredients and steam it in a steamer for 1 hour.

Directions   Take it warmly.

Indications   Nourishing the yin and clear the heat, moistening the lung and arrest the cough. It is applied to cough, low fever and night sweat.

Recipe 1
Ingredients

edible bird's nest   5 g

root of American ginseng (*Radix Panacis Quinquefolii*)   5 g

Process   Soak the edible bird's nest in water, clean it up, then let it dry, put it in bowl, add in the root of American ginseng and right amount of water, steam it over water in a steamer for 3 hours.

Directions   Take the decoction once daily.

Indications   Nourishing the yin and moistening the dryness. Cough and night sweat due to deficiency of lung and stomach yin.

Recipe 2
Ingredients

lean pork	50 g
apricot kernel (*Semen Armeniacae*)	10 g
glehnia root (*Radix Glehniae*)	15 g

Process   Decoct all them in water.

Directions   Take it twice daily.

Indications   Nourishing the lung and removing the phlegm, promoting the production of body fluid. It is applied for the prolonged cough with few phlegm, thirst and dry and itching in throat.

Recipe 3
Ingredients
edible bird's nest	10 g
tremella (*Tremella*)	15 g
crystal sugar	right amount

Process　Clean the edible bird's nest with water, then soak it with hot water for 3 to 4 hours, then get rid of the feather, soak it in hot water for another hour; soak the tremlle in hot water for 1 hour, put all them in a bowl and steam it over water in a steamer.

Directions　Take it once daily.

Indications　Replenishing the deficiency, nourishing the lung-yin. It's applied to the cough and night sweat.

Recipe 4
Ingredients
mutton liver	60 g
sesame oil	30 g
salt	right amount

Process　Cut the liver of goat into slices, heat the sesame oil in a pot, when it is 80 per cent boil, add the slices and stir-fry them for a while.

Directions　Take the mutton once daily.

Indications　Moistening the lung and arrest the cough.

Internal Diseases

It's applied to prolonged cough.

Recipe 5
Ingredients
    tremella (*tremella*)   15 g
    crystal sugar   25 g
    duck egg   1

Process   Decoct the tremella and crystal sugar in right amount of water, when it come to boil beat the duck egg in it.

Directions   Take it twice daily.

Indications   Nourishing the lung and arrest the cough. It's applied to cough with phlegm due to deficiency of yin and dryness of lung.

Recipe 6
Ingredients
    edible bird's nest   5 g
    white pear (*Malum Piri*)   2
    Sichuan fritillary bulb (*Bulb Fritillariae Cirrhosae*)   10 g
    crystal sugar   5 g

Process   Get rid of the stone of white pear and put other ingredients in the hole of pear, then cover it well, put it in a bowl and steam it over water in steamer.

Directions   Take the pear once daily.

Indications Nourishing the yin and moistening the dryness, arrest the cough and remove the phlegm. It's applied to prolonged cough with short breath and lassitude.

Recipe 7
Ingredients
edible bird's nest	10 g
round - polished glutinous rice (*Semen Oryzae Sativae*)	100 g
crystal sugar	50 g

Process Soak the edible bird's nest in warm water, clean it up, and go on soak it in boiling water; Decoct 100 g rice in 3 bowls of water over a strong fire, when it comes to boil, then heat it over a slow fire, add the edible bird's nest in it and cooking it for about an hour, add in the crystal sugar in it.

Directions Take the mixture once daily.

Indications Nourishing the lung and moistening the yin, arresting cough and remove phlegm. It is applied to prolonged cough due to deficiency of the lung.

Recipe 8
Ingredients
jellyfish	80 g
white radish (*Napus*)	

decoct them in 3 bowls of water until half and a bowl of

decoction left.

Directions   Take it in twice and one dose daily for 2 weeks successively.

Indications   Moistening lung, arresting cough and remove asthma. It is applied to prolonged cough and chronic bronchitis.

Chapter One

SECTION 3 Chronic Bronchitis

Chronic bronchitis causes increased mucous secretion in the tracheobronchial tract, resulting in a productive cough which is present on most days for a minimum of three months of the year and for at least two consecutive years. It is the most common debilitating respiratory disease in China as well as in other countries, particularly among the aged.

Its cause is not yet clear, but several factors are strongly associated with this disease. **Cigarette smoking** has been shown to be the most important predisposing factor. Some doctors hold that *pneumococci* and *hemophilus* cause infections that result in chronic bronchitis. However, others believe that the infections are the result rather than the cause of this chronic disease. Endogenous factors may also be involved. A genetic abnormality that affects mucus production may impair bronchial clearance and harm protective mechanisms, leading to recurrent or chronic infection. Bronchial allergies may increase secretion of mucus or cause one to be more susceptible to bronchial infection. Exposure to cold exacerbates the condition and may also be related to constitutional hypersensitivity.

Goblet cells in the epithelial lining and bronchial mucous glands lying beneath the epithelium produce the secretion of the tracheobronchial trees. In chronic bronchitis, the mucous glands increase in thickness, and goblet cells increase in number. These changes, along with an increase in the volume of tracheobronchial secretions, explain the chronic productive cough. But late in the course of chronic bronchitis, severe airway obstruction usually occurs, and this cannot be entirely explained by the narrowing of central airways caused by mucous gland thickening and obstruction by the secretions themselves. Small airway obstruction resulting from goblet cell proliferation or bronchiolitis may play an important role. Other morphologic changes accompanying goblet cell and bronchial gland abnormalities include fragmentation of the mucosa, destruction of cilia, inflammatory cell infiltration of the epithelium and subepithelium and basal cell hyperplasia and squamous metaplasia of columnar epithelium. Once ciliated mucosae have been disrupted, airway defense becomes more susceptible to subsequent injury.

Owing to the complexity of its pathogenesis and pathological changes, chronic bronchitis is difficult to treat, especially where a long-term cure is concerned.

In traditional Chinese medicine, chronic bronchitis is closely linked to *cough*, *phlegm* and *dyspnea* in syndrome diagnosis and treatment.

Chapter One

ETIOLOGY AND PATHOGENESIS

The hallmarks of chronic bronchitis are a chronic cough and sputum production. Shortness of breath may later become prominent. From the traditional point of view, cough is a common symptom of lung disease, but the production of sputum is not necessarily confined to disorders of the lungs. Purulent sputum usually results when exogenous pathogenic factors, particularly heat, attack the lungs. Production of nonpurulent voluminous phlegm is often attributed to dysfunction of the spleen. In this case, the lungs merely store the phlegm and cough it up. Accumulation of phlegm in the lungs renders them vulnerable to repeated attacks by exogenous pathogenic factors, resulting in acute exacerbations. Shortness of breath with difficulty in exhalation, usually occurring late in the course of chronic bronchitis indicates that the kidneys are involved, since they help the lungs respire, and protracted difficulty in respiration with prolonged exhalation is characteristic of impaired kidneys.

In summary, traditional Chinese medicine considers chronic bronchitis a disease of the lungs that also involves impairment of the functions of the spleen and the kidneys. Only during acute exacerbations do exogenous pathogens play an important role.

MAIN POINTS OF DIAGNOSIS

1. Productive cough is present on most days for a minimum of 3 months in the year (in at least two consecutive years).

2. During relatively quiescent period, the only finding may be increased anteroposterior diameter of the chest. Other findings such as hyperresonance to percussion, prolonged expiratory phase, scattered diffuse coarse or moderate rhonchi and rale and wheezing are also present.

3. Chest x-ray shows evidence of pulmonary overinflation with increased anteroposterior diameter, flattened diaphragm and increased retrosternal air space. There often prominent and increased bronchial markings at the lung base as parallel or tapering shadows (*tram lines*) which reflect the increased thickness of the bronchial wall.

Recipe 1
Ingredients

fresh shaddock	500 g
honey (*Mel*)	250 g
spirits	right amount

Process Get rid of the stone of orange and cut it into cubes, soak them in right amount of spirit in a jar over night. Take them out, decoct them in right amount of water until it become sticky, add in the honey and mix them well.

Directions　Take it three times daily and 3 g each time.
Indications　Chronic bronchitis.

Recipe 2
Ingredients

Radish (*Napus*)	500 g
bite apricot kernel (*Semen Armeniacae*)	15 g
pork lung	250 g
salt	right amount

Process　Cut the radish into cubes, get rid of the tip of apricot kernel, clean the pig's lung and soak it in boiling water for a while, decoct all them it in right amount of water in a tile, then season it with salt.

Directions　Eat pork lung and drink the soup. 2 – 3 doses weekly for 4 weeks successively.

Indications　Chronic bronchitis.

Recipe 3
Ingredients

fresh water chestnut (*Bulbus Heleocharis Tuberosae*)	15 g
jellyfish	30 g
Sichuan fritillary bulb (*Bulb Fritillariae Cirrhosae*)	9 g

Process　Get rid of the peel of chestnut, soak the jellyfish in water, clean it up and cut it into pieces, decoct all the ingredients in right amount of water over a slow fire for an hour.

Directions Eat the chestnut and jellyfish, drink the soup. Take it in twice daily for a week successively.

Indications Chronic bronchitis.

Recipe 4

Ingredients

chicken bile	3
white sugar	right amount

Process Get the bile of chicken and mix it with sugar.

Directions Take it twice daily, one course of administration consists of 5 days.

Indications Clearing away heat, removing heat and arresting asthma. It is applied to chronic bronchitis, cough and asthma.

Recipe 5

Ingredients

lucid ganoderma (*Ganoderma Lucidum*)	15 g
glehnia root (*Radix Glehniae*)	20 g
lily bulb (*Bulbus Lilii*)	15 g

Process Decoct all them in right amount of water.

Directions Take the decoction once daily.

Indications Nourishing the yin and clearing the lung. It

is applicable to chronic bronchitis.

Recipe 6

Ingredients

crystal sugar	150 g
edible bird's nest	30 g
wolfberry fruit (*Fructus Lycii*)	15 g

Process Soak the edible bird's nest in warm water, clean it up, put it in a bowl, add right amount of water, then steam it over water in a steamer, ladle it out; put crystal sugar and wolfberry in a big bowl, add in right amount of water, steam it over water in a steamer for half an hour, mix it with edible bird's nest well.

Directions Take it once daily.

Indications Nourishing lung, replenishing yin, clearing the lung and remove phlegm. It is applicable to chronic bronchitis, asthma and pulmonary tuberculosis.

SECTION 4   Bronchial Asthma

Bronchial asthma is an allergic respiratory disease with recurrent attacks. Patients with asthma usually have a history of exudative conditions such as eczema, urticaria and angioneurotic edema. It is more commonly seen in children of four or five. Once they are exposed to allergens like bacterial or viral infection, flower powder, mites and dust, or after they take in fish, shrimps and protein, asthmatic attacks may occur. It may be often induced by sudden changes of the weather, overwork and mental irritation. Asthma is more common in spring and autumn, being prone to occur repeatedly. In infants and young children, it appears mostly like asthmatic bronchitis. With the growth of the children the frequency of attacks gradually reduces and the disease is even relieved. But when they grow older, the disease will reoccur. It is difficult to cure completely, usually becoming a life – long disorder.

Chapter One

ETIOLOGY AND PATHOGENESIS

Bronchial asthma results when exopathic factors act on the endopathic factors. The patient is generally weak in constitution and deficient in the functions of the lung, spleen and kidney. The deficiency of the lung may result in retention of water, the dysfunction of the spleen in water transportation, and deficiency of kidney in activating qi to promote diuresis. Retention and accumulation of water and dampness form turbid sputum, which stores in the interior. As a result, the sick child usually manifested by exudative conditions, showing pale complexion, fatness, recurrent eczema, loose muscle, and rumbling sound of the sputum in the throat, etc..

Because of the deficiency of lung - energy, the **yang** of the defensive function fails to strengthen the striae, which in turn makes one subject to attacks of exogenous pathogenic factors. In this case, if there are sudden changes of weather, the invasion of exopathogens into the body, the exposure to some substances, such as flower powder, mites, parasites and dust, irregular diet, over - eating of uncooked, cold, salty and acid food or taking in fish, shrimps and protein, the latent phlegm will be irritated, obstructing the air passage, making lung - qi unable to go up and down, therefore causing sudden attacks of asthma. Asthma that is due to retention of cold-type phlegm in the interior caused by the attack of wind-cold evil, internal injury by improper diet or deficiency of **yang** is known as cold-type asthma. Asthma that is due to deficiency of **yin**, accumulation of phlegm-heat in the lung or the transformation of cold-type phlegm into heat is known as heat-type asthma. If recurrent attacks of asthma further injure the vital essence of the lung, spleen and the kidney, the disease may present as deficient-type asthma with shortness of breath, bronchial wheezing when moving, and productive cough, which are commonly seen at the remission stage of the disease. Because the disease is caused by deficiency in origin and excess in superficiality, or a deficiency syndrome complicated with excess, it is difficult to be completely cured. When weather suddenly changes, diet is improper, and the mental irritated, the combination of exopathogens and endopathogens leads to recurrent attacks of asthma.

MAIN POINTS OF DIAGNOSIS

Bronchial asthma is divided into two different stages: attack and remission.

1. Typical Attack: It is marked by sudden onset or by the presymptoms of stuffy nose, sneezing, itching in the throat and oppressed feeling in the chest followed by asthma, shortness of breath, dyspnea, sound of sputum in thethroat,

restlessness, failure of horizontal position, pale complexion, cyanosis of the lips and fingers, and cold sweat on the forehead. At beginning, there is dry cough, and later, the amount of sputum graduallyincreases. Once the sputum is removed, the attack will be relieved. The duration of the attack varies from a few minutes to several hours. A fewchildren are found in status asthmaticus.

2. **Signs:** Stethoscope examination finds obvious diminution of respiration in the two lungs, prolonged expiratory phase and wheezing all over the two lungs. In chronic patients, drumstick finger and barrel chest are commonly seen.

3. **X－ray Examination:** X－ray examination of the chest reveals changes ofemphysema. When secondary infection occurs, patchy shadows can be observed.

4. **Laboratory Test:** White cell count and neutrophilic granulocytesare generally normal; eosinophilic granulocytes increase by more than 5%; whensecondary infection presents, white cell count and neutrophilic granulocytes mayincrease.

Recipe 1
Ingredients
    tortoise blood   right amount
    white sugar   right amount
Process   Mix them well and infuse it with boiling wa-

ter.

Directions   Take it once daily and 3 spoon of it for each time.

Indications   Nourishing the yin and replenishing blood, arresting cough and removing asthma. It is applicable to chronic bronchitis, cough.

Recipe 2
Ingredients

carp	1
polished glutinous rice (*Semen Oryzae Glutinosae*)	200 g

Process   Get rid of the scales, wrap it with wet paper and toast it over fire., get rid its bone and grind it into fine powder, make it into gruel with rice and right amount of water.

Directions   Take it before meal.
Indications   Chronic bronchitis.

Recipe 3
Ingredients

bile of yellow croaker	1
hawthorn fruit (*Fructus Crataegi*)	50 g
root of tea tree	50 g
Chinese-date (*Fructus Ziziphi Jujubae*)	5

Process   Decoct all them in right amount of water.

Directions   Take it one dose daily.
Indications   Chronic bronchitis.

Recipe 4
Ingredients
grapefruit	1
black bone silky fowl	1

Process   Cut open the grapefruit and remove the segment; kill the black bone silky fowl, get rid of the feather and entrails, cut it into small cubes, put them in the cave of the grapefruit, add in right amount of water, seal it and wrap it with earth, toast it over a fire of wood for 5 – 6 hours, when it is done, remove the earth.

Directions   Eat the meat and drink the soup. Once weekly and take it until the patient is cured.

Indications   Chronic bronchitis.

Recipe 5
Ingredients
ginseng (*Radix Ginseng*)	6 g
walnut kernel (*Semen Juglandis*)	6 g

Process   Decoct all them in right amount of water.
Directions   Take it twice or three times daily.
Indications   Chronic bronchitis and prolonged cough due to deficiency of lung and kidney.

Recipe 6
Ingredients
   donkey－hide gelatin（Colla Corii Asini）
                                             15 g
   apricot kernel（Semen Armeniacae）   10 g
   birthwort   10 g
   polished glutinous rice（Semen Oryzae Glutinosae）   30 g
   crystal sugar   right amount

Process Decoct apricot kernel and birthwort in water, sift out the decoction and make it into gruel with rice, then heat the donkey－hide gelatin melt and add it in the gruel. When it is nearly done, add in the crystal sugar and go on cooking for a while.

Directions Take it warmly.

Indications Replenishing the middle－jiao and arresting cough. It is applicable to asthma.

Recipe 7
Ingredients
   ginseng（Radix Ginseng）   3－5 g
   poria（Poria）   15 g
   walnut kernel（Semen Juglandis）   10 g
   gecko powder（Pulvis Gecko）   5 g
   ginger（Zingiberis）   5 g
   polished round－grained rice（Semen Oryzae Sati-

vae) 100 g

Process　Decoct the ginseng, poria and powder of geeko in right amount of water in an earthenware pot, when it is nearly done, add in the slices of ginger and go on cooking for a while, then sift out the decoction from the dregs; pound the walnut kernel into mash and extract its juice. Make the rice into thin gruel with the juice, decoction and right amount of water.

Directions　Take the gruel once daily.

Indications　Prompting the production of body fluid and arresting cough. It is applicable to the cough and deficiency of lung.

Recipe 8

Ingredients

　　lucid ganoderma (*Ganoderma Licidum*) 10 g
　　pinellia tuber (*Rhizoma Pinelliae*) 3 g
　　perilla leaf (*Folium Perillae*) 10 g
　　magnolia bark (*Cortex Magnoliae Officinalis*)
　　　　　　　　　　　　　　　　　　　5 g
　　poria (*Poria*) 15 g
　　crystal sugar 15 g

Process　Decoct all the ingredients in right amount of water.

Directions　Take it in two or three times daily.

Internal Diseases

Indications　Clearing away heat and arrest the asthma. It is applicable to asthma.

SECTION 5 Pulmonary Tuberculosis

Pulmonary tuberculosis is an infectious disease due to infection of *tuberculosis bacillus* through the respiratory tract. It is classified into two types: primary and secondary and mainly manifested by cough, expectoration, hemoptysis, chest pain, tidal fever, night sweat and emaciation. It belongs to the category of *consumptive disease of the lung* in traditional Chinese medicine.

ETIOLOGY AND PATHOGENESIS

Tuberculosis bacillus attacks the lung and causes this disease when vital − qi is deficient. At the early stage, yin − fluid is usually exhausted and only the lung is involved. Following that, there occurs hyperactivity of fire due to yin − deficiency and both the lung and kidney are involved together with the heart and liver. Or both the spleen and lung are involved and both qi and yin are deficient. At the advanced stage, deficiency of yin affects yang, resulting in deficiency of both yin and yang. In the whole course, yin − deficiency is of the most importance.

Recipe 1
Ingredients

pseudostellaria root（*Radix Pseudostellariae*）	120 g
glehnia root（*Radix Glehniae*）	120 g
fragrant solomonseal rhizome（*Rhizoma Polygonati Odorati*）	120 g
Chinese yam（*Rhizoma Dioscoreae*）	120 g
poria（*Poria*）	120 g
lucid asparagus	120 g
apricot kernel（*Semen Armeniacae*）	120 g
fresh rehmannia root	120 g
prepared rehmannia root	
fresh liquorice（*Radix Glycyrrhizae*）	60 g
aster root（*Radix Asteris*）	60 g
lily bulb（*Bulbus Lilii*）	60 g
schisandra fruit（*Fructus Schisandrae*）	30 g
Sichuan fritillary bulb（*Bulb Fritillariae Cirrhosae*）	30 g
white cogongrass rhizome（*Rhizoma Imperatae*）	240 g

Process Decoct all them in water twice, sift out the decoctions, mix the decoctions well. Heat the crystal sugar in a pot until it is melt, add in the decoction and go on cooking until it is become sticky extract, put it in a china bottle and seal it well. Put the bottle in earth for 7 days.

Directions Infuse a spoonful sticky extract with boiling water, take it three times daily.

Indications Pulmonary tuberculosis.

Recipe 2
Ingredients

cinnabar (*Cinnabaris*)	20 g
realgar	10 g
orpiment	10 g
musk (*Moschus*)	1 g

Process Grind all them into fine powder. Cut 1/3 of a garlic. Rub the spinal column from **Dàzhuī** (**DU**14) to **Chángqiáng** (**DU**1) with the garlic on which surface the powder of the ingredients are glued. The treating area should reveal red swelling and pain.

Directions Apply the treatment once daily.
Indications Pulmonary tuberculosis.

Recipe 3
Ingredients

glehnia root (*Radix Glehniae*)	10 g
ophiopogon root (*Radix Ophiopogonis*)	10 g
lily bulb (*Bulbus Lilii*)	10 g
fritillary bulb (*Bulbus Fritillariae*)	10 g

polished round – grained rice (*Semen Oryzae Sativae*)
　　　　　　　　　　　　　　　　　　　50 g
　　crystal sugar　　　　　　　　right amount

Process　Decoct first four ingredients into fine powder and decoct all them in right amount of water over a slow fire for an hour, sift out the decoction from dregs, add in rice and make it into thin gruel, when it is nearly done, add in the crystal sugar and go on cooking for a while. Grind fritillaria bulb into fine powder.

Directions　Infuse the fine powder with the boiling gruel, take it twice or three times daily.

Indications　Pulmonary tuberculosis.

Recipe 4

Ingredients

　　donkey – hide gelatin (*Colla Corii Asini*)
　　　　　　　　　　　　　　　　　　　30 g
　　polished glutinous rice (*Semen Oryzae Glutinosae*)
　　　　　　　　　　　　　　　　　　　100 g
　　brown sugar　　　　　　　　right amount

Process　Make the rice into gruel, pound the donkey – hide gelatine into mash, when the gruel is nearly done, add in the powder of the donkey – hide gelatine and go on cooking with stir, it will be done after it come to 2 or 3 boils. Add in right amount of sugar in it.

Directions　Take the gruel once daily.

Indications　Pulmonary tuberculosis with prolonged cough.

Recipe 5
Ingredients
  lily bulb（*Bulbus Lilii*）   60 g
  polished round - grained rice（*Semen Oryzae Sativae*）   100 g
  honey（*Mel*）   30 g

Process　Make the lily bulb and rice into gruel with water, when it is nearly done, add in the honey.

Directions　Take the gruel once daily.

Indications　Pulmonary tuberculosis.

Recipe 6
Ingredients
  edible bird's nest   10 g
  tremella（*tremella*）   20 g
  crystal sugar   right amount

Process　Soak the edible bird's nest and tremella in water until they become soft and enlarged, add in crystal sugar and steam it over water in a steamer.

Directions　Take it once daily.

Indications　Pulmonary tuberculosis with the cough, night sweat, dryness of mouth and lassitude.

Internal Diseases

SECTION 6 Chronic Gastritis

Recipe 1
Ingredients

　　Chinese yam (Rhizoma Dioscoreae)
　　mutton
　　polished round-grained rice (Semen Oryzae Sativae)

　　　salt, slices of ginger, gourmet right amount for each

Process　Grind the mutton and Chinese yam into mash. Make them and rice into gruel, when it is done, season it with condiments.

Directions　Take the gruel once daily.

Indications　Chronic gastritis.

Recipe 2
Ingredients

　　pig's large intestine　　　　　　　　　　1
　　sesame oil, thick sauce, and threads of ginger
　　　　　　　　　　right amount for each

Process Clear the large intestine, decoct it in water until it is done, ladle it out and cut it into sections, stir-fry it with the condiments.

Directions Take it with other foods and take it for five doses successively.

Indications vomiting and poor appetite.

Recipe 3
Ingredients

red sage root (*Radix Salviae Miltiorrhizae*)

                                  25 g
sandal wood   15 g
prepared liquorice (*Radix Glycyrrhizae*) 10 g
honey (*Mel*)   50 g

Process Decoct the first ingredients in right amount of water, sift out the decoction from the dregs, add in the honey.

Directions Take it one dose daily.

Indications Gastric ulcer and chronic gastritis with abdominal pain.

Recipe 4
Ingredients

stone of longan (*Semen Longan*)

                                    right amount

Process Bake it dry and grind it into fine powder.

Directions   Take it with boiled water twice daily, 25 g for each time.

Indications   Acute gastroenteritis.

Recipe 5
Ingredients
   milk half bound
   quail egg (*Coturnix*)   1

Process   Heat the milk until it come to boil, heat the quail egg in it and go on cooking for a boil.

Directions   Take it before breakfast once daily.

Indications   Chronic gastroenteritis.

Recipe 6
Ingredients
   dangshen (*Radix Codonopsis Pilosulae*)   45 g
   poria (*Poria*)   45 g
   germinated barley (*Fructus Hordei Germinatus*)
                                              45 g
   rice sprout (*Fructus Oryzae Germinatus*)
                                              45 g
   scutellaria root (*Radix Scutellariae*)   36 g
   red sage root (*Radix Salviae Miltiorrhizae*)
                                              36 g
   fragrant solomonseal rhizome (*Rhizoma Polygonati Odorati*)   36 g

white atractylodes rhizome (*Rhizoma Atractylodis Macrocephalae*)　27 g
dried orange peel (*Pericarpium Citri*)　27 g
aucklandia root (*Radix Aucklandiae*)　27 g
agastache (*Herba Pogostemonis seu Agastachis*)　27 g
amomum fruit (*Fructus Amomi*)　27 g
Chinese yam (*Rhizoma Dioscoreae*)　27 g
white peony root (*Radix Paeoniae Alba*)　27 g
magnolia bark (*Cortex Magnoliae Officinalis*)　27 g
hawthorn fruit (*Fructus Crataegi*)　27 g
medicated leaven (*Massa Fermentata Medicinalis*)　27 g
pinellia tuber (*Rhizoma Pinelliae*)　20 g
prepared liquorice (*Radix Glycyrrhizae*)　20 g

Process　Decoct all them in right amount of boil water for 15 minutes, sift out the decoction; add the right amount of water in dregs, and decoct it in water for 20 minutes, sift out the decoction from dregs, mix the decoctions well.

Directions　Take it in twice, one dose daily.

Indications　Chronic gastritis.

Recipe 7
Ingredients

> *ginger* (*Zingiberis*) 30 g
> *tangerine peel* (*Pericarpium Citri Reticulatae*)
> 10 g
> *black pepper* (*Fructus Pipperis Nigri*) 3 g
> *crucian carp* 1

Process Get rid of the scales and entrails, wrap other ingredients with gauze cloth, put it in the cave of fish, decoct it in right amount of water, when it is done, season it with salt.

Directions Eat the fish and drink the soup.

Indications Chronic gastritis.

SECTION 7 Peptic Ulcer

Peptic ulcer is divided into gastric and duodenal ulcer. The disease is closely related to the acidity of gastric juice and the digestion of enzymes. It is mainly marked by regular pain in the upper abdomen. In cases of gastric ulcer, postprandial pain is most frequently complained of. It manifests regularly as 1) food-intake, 2) pain, and 3) remission. It is hunger pain that is commonly seen in cases with duodenal ulcer. The pain is marked by 1) hunger, 2) pain, 3) food-intake, and 4) remission regularly. Or the pain occurs at midnight. The accompanying symptoms may be eructation, sour regurgitation, nausea, vomiting, and even hematemesis. Peptic ulcer belongs to the categories of "Wèi wǎn tòng", "Xīn tòng", etc. in traditional Chinese medicine.

Recipe 1
Ingredients
jellyfish   500 g
Chinese-date (*Fructus Ziziphi Jujubae*)
                                                        500 g

brown sugar   250 g

Process   Decoct all them in right amount of water until it becomes sticky jelly.

Directions   Take it one spoon of it each time, twice daily.

Indications   Moisturize bowels by clearing away dry-heat. For gastroduodenal ulcer.

Recipe 2

Ingredients

powder of amomum fruit (*Fructus Amomi*)
                                                       10 g

pork tripe   1

pepper powder, prickly ash peel, scallion, ginger, lard, salt and millet wine right amount for each

Process   Clean the pig's stomach and cut it into slices, then decoct it in water. When it come to boil, remove the float, season it with condiments and go on cooking it over a slow fire to get a thick soup.

Directions   Eat the meat and drink the soup.

Indications   Gastroduodenal ulcer and chronic gastroenteritis with anorexia.

Recipe 3

Ingredients

milk   250 g

honey (*Mel*)   50 g
powder of hyacinth bletilla (*Rhizoma Bletillae*)
                                                               10 g

Process   Heat the milk in a pot, when it come to boil, then add the honey and white mustard seed powder.

Directions   Take it once daily.

Indications   Gastroduodenal ulcer.

Recipe 4

Ingredients

cuttlebone	50 g
egg shell	50 g
sesame oil	50 g
white sugar	50 g

Process   Bake the first three ingredients dry and grind them into fine powder, then mix with white sugar well.

Directions   Take the fine powder three times daily, 15 g for each time.

Indications   Gastroduodenal ulcer.

Recipe 5

Ingredients

egg shell   50

cuttle bone (*Os Sepiellae seu Sepiae*)   50 g

Chicken's gizzard - membrane (*Endothelium Corneum Gigeriae Galli*)   20 g

    parched litchi seed (*Semen Litchi*)   10 g
    parched long pepper (*Fructus Piperis Longi*)
                                                              10 g
    parched galangal rhizome (*Rhizoma Alpiniae Officinarum*)   10 g
    parched finger of citron (*Fructus Citri Sarcodactyli*)   10 g
    hyacinth bletilla (*Rhizoma Bletillae*)   10 g
    liquorice (*Radix Glycyrrhizae*)   10 g

Process   Grind all them into fine powder, and mix them well.

Directions   Take it with warm boiled water three times daily, 1 – 2 g each time. One course of treatment consists of 30 doses. There is an interval of one week between two courses.

Indications   Gastroduodenal ulcer.

Recipe 6

Ingredients

    tangerine peel (*Pericarpium Citri Reticulatae*)
                                                              15 g
    polished round – grained rice (*Semen Oryzae Sativae*)   100 g
    white sugar   right amount

Process   Clean the orange peel up and decoct it in water

for 20 minutes, then sift out the decoction, make the rice into gruel with the decoction and right amount of water, when it is done, add in the sugar and mix them well.

    Directions   Take it once a time, one dose daily.
    Indications   Gastroduodenal ulcer.

SECTION 8 Hepatitis

Recipe 1
Ingredients
  Chinese yam（*Rhizoma Dioscoreae*）　　30 g
  longan（*Arillus Longan*）　　20 g
  soft－shelled turtle（*Trioyx Sinensis*）
　　　　　　　　　　1（about 500 g）

Process　Kill the soft－shelled turtle, get rid of its entrails and clean it up, then decoct it and Chinese yam and litchi in water until it is well done.

Directions　Eat the meat and drink the soup.

Indications　Nourishing the yin and replenishing the yang. It is applicable to cirrhosis of the liver, chronic hepatitis, and hepatosplenomegaly.

Recipe 2
Ingredients
  schisandra fruit（*Fructus Schisandrae*）400 g

red sage root (*Radix Salviae Miltiorrhizae*)
                                                400 g
isatis root (*Radix Isatidis*)   200 g
honey (*Mel*)   750 g

Process   Grind all the ingredients into fine powder, then mix them with honey to make boluses, 10 g for each bolus.

Directions   Take it three times daily, 1 – 2 boluses for each time.

Indications   Chronic virus hepatitis.

Recipe 3
Ingredients
    astragalus root (*Radix astragali seu Hedysari*)
                                         15 – 30 g
    pseudostellaria root (*Radix Pseudostellariae*)
                                         15 – 30 g
    poria (*Poria*)   15 – 30 g
    giant knotweed   15 – 30 g
    phellodendron bark (*Cortex Phellodendri*)
                                       15 – 30 g
    red sage root (*Radix Salviae Miltiorrhizae*)
                                         10 – 30 g
    hawthorn fruit (*Fructus Crataegi*)   10 – 30 g
    loranthus mulberry mistletoe (*Ramulus Loranthis*)   10 – 30 g

Internal Diseases

  Siberian solomonseal rhizome（*Rhizoma Polygonati*） 10 - 30 g
  white atractylodes rhizome（*Rhizoma Atractylodis Macrocephalae*） 10 - 15 g
  subprostrate sophora root（*Radix Sophorae Subprostrate*） 10 - 15 g
  cinnamon twig（*Ramulus Cinnamomi*）
    3 - 15 g
  dried ginger（*Rhizoma Zingiberis*） 3 - 15 g
  coix seed（*Semen Coicis*） 15 - 40 g
Process Decoct all the ingredients in water.
Directions Take it in three times, one dose daily.
Indications Hepatitis B carriers.

Recipe 4
Ingredients
  walnut kernel（*Semen Juglandis*） 1000 g
  sesame seed（*Semen Sesami Nigrum*） 1000 g
  Chinese - date（*Fructus Ziziphi Jujubae*）
    1000 g
  fresh - water turtle shell（*Carapax Trionycis*）
    60 g
  Sichuan fritillary bulb（*Bulb Fritillariae Cirrhosae*） 6 g
  poria（*Poria*） 60 g
  Chicken's gizzard - membranae（*Endothelium*

Corneum Gigeriae Galli) 30 g

Process   Bake the Sichuan fritillary bulb, poria, fresh-water turtle shell, membrane of chicken's gizzard dry and grind them into fine powder separately, Parch the black sesame and grind it into fine powder, pound the walnut kernel into fine powder, steam the Chinese-date over water, and get rid of its stone, make all them into boluses with honey, 10 g for each bolus.

Directions   Take it three times daily, one bolus for each time.

Indications   Chronic hepatitis with symptoms of hypochondriac pain and constipation, etc..

Recipe 5

Ingredients

white poria（*Poria*）	20 g
red phaseolus bean（*Semen Phaseoli*）	50 g
coix seed（*Semen Coicis*）	100 g

Process   Soak the red phaseolus bean in water for 6 hours, then stew it with the rice in water. When red phaseolus bean is well done, add the powder of the poria and go on cooking to make a gruel, season it with sugar.

Directions   Take it several times daily.

Indications   Invigorate the spleen and remove damp-heat, clear away heat as the detoxification. Indicated for jaundice of damp- heat type.

Recipe 6
Ingredients

millet vinegar	1000 g
fresh pork bone	500 g
brown sugar	120 g
white sugar	120 g

Process Decoct the pork bone, white sugar and brown sugar in vinegar until it has boiled for 30 minutes. Sift out the decoction.

Directions Take it three times daily after meals, 30 – 40 ml for adult and 10 – 15 ml for children. One administration course consists of 1 month.

Indications Chronic and acute hepatitis. Contraindicated for cases with high fever.

Recipe 7
Ingredients

kelp (*Thallus Laminariae*)	25 g
litchi seed (*Semen Litchi*)	15 g
aniseed (*Fructus Foeniculi*)	15 g
green tangerine peel (*Pericarpium Citri Reticulatae Viride*)	15 g

Process Decoct all them in right amount of water.

Directions Take it once daily.

Indications Relieve the masses by soothing the liver.

Indicated for hepatosplenomegaly.

Recipe 8
Ingredients
 eel   3
 reed rhizome (*Rhizoma Phragmitis*) 30 g
 loranthus mulberry mistletoe (*Ramulus Loranthis*) 60 g
 cooking oil, *salt* right amount for each

Process Get rid of the eel's entrails, cut it into sections and clean them up, decoct them and reed rhizome and loranthus mulberry mistletoe in water, season it with cooking oil and salt.

Directions Eat the meat and drink the soup.
Indications Chronic hepatitis.

Recipe 9
Ingredients
 Chinese angelica root (*Radix Angelicae Sinensis*) 15 g
 dangshen (*Radix Codonopsis Pilosulae*) 15 g
 hen   1
 Scallion   right amount
 ginger   right amount
 millet wine   right amount
 salt   right amount

Internal Diseases

Process　Kill the hen and cut it open, get rid of it feather and entrails, clean it up. Put the dangshen and Chinese angelica root in the cave of hen, put it in an earthenware pot, add in right amount of water, ginger, scallion, millet wine, salt. Heat it over a strong fire, when it come to boil, heat it over a slow fire until it is well done.

Directions　Eat the meat and drink the soup. Take it in several times.

Indications　Chronic hepatitis and anemia due to deficiency of blood of the liver and kidney.

Recipe 10

Ingredients

　　gentian root（*Radix Gentianae*）　　1.8 g
　　vinegar bupleurum root（*Radix Bupleuri*）
　　　　　　　　　　　　　　　　　　1.8 g
　　Chuanxiong Rhizome（*Rhizoma Ligustici Chuanxiong*）　　1.8 g
　　chrysanthemum（*Flos Chrysanthemi*）　　3 g
　　rehmannia root（*Radix Rehmanniae*）　　3 g

Process　Grind all them into fine powder, then decoct them in water.

Directions　Take it as drink. one dose daily.

Indications　Hepatitis, cholecystitis, acute conjunctivitis.

Chapter One

Recipe 11

Ingredients

day lily (*Flos Hemerocallis*)   10 g
raw liquorice (*Radix Glycyrrhizae*)   8 g
schisandra fruit (*Fructus Schisandrae*)   5 g
Chinese-date (*Fructus Ziziphi Jujubae*)

  60 g

Process   Soak all them in boiling water for 5 minutes.

Directions   Take it as drink, one dose daily.

Indications   Hepatitis B, chronic active hepatitis, icterohepatitis.

Recipe 12

Ingredients

lucid ganoderma (*Ganoderma Licidum*)

  10 – 12 g

glossy privet fruit (*Fructus Ligustri Lucidi*)

  15 g

red sage root (*Radix Salviae Miltiorrhizae*)

  9 g

Chicken's gizzard-membrane (*Endothelium Corneum Gigeriae Galli*)   9 g

Process   Decoct all them in water for an hour, then sift out the decoction from dregs; add the water in the dregs and decoct it again and sift out the decoction, then mix the decoctions together.

Internal Diseases

Directions   Take the decoctions in twice daily, both in the morning and in the evening, one dose daily.

Indications   Invigorating liver and kidney, promoting blood circulation and digestion. Chronic hepatitis of the type of deficiency of both liver and kidney marked by hypochondriac pain, little food − intake, anorexia, lassitude and fatigue, etc..

Recipe 13
Ingredients
fresh − water turtle shell (*Carapax Trionycis*)
15 g
jujube (*Fructus Ziziphi Jujubae*)   10
vinegar   2 spoons
white sugar half spoon

Process   Dissolve the sugar in the vinegar; clean the Chinese − date up for latter use. Stir − fry the fresh − water turtle shell in a hot pot for 5 minutes, then add in the vinegar and stir − fry it with stir, when the juice it nearly dry add the Chinese − date and a bowl of water, stew it over a slow fire for 1 hour. When the Chinese − date is well done, remove the fresh − water turtle shell.

Directions   Eat the Chinese − date and drink the soup. One course consists of 2 months.

Indications   Hepatitis.

Recipe 14

Ingredients

astragalus root（*Radix astragali seu Hedysari*）	30 g
pueraria root（*Radix Puerariae*）	30 g
wolfberry fruit（*Fructus Lycii*）	12 g
platycodon root（*Radix Platycodi*）	12 g
trichosanthes fruit（*Fructus Trichosanthis*）	20 g
red sage root（*Radix Salviae Miltiorrhizae*）	20 g
white peony root（*Radix Paeoniae Alba*）	15 g
hawthorn fruit（*Fructus Crataegi*）	15 g
cat－tail pollen（*Pollen Typhae*）	10 g
feces of flying squirrel	10 g
notoginseng（*Radix Notoginseng*）	1.5 g
powder of bufflo horn	2 g

Process　　Decoct the first ten ingredients in water and sift out the decoction, infuse the flour of the notoginseng and fine powder of bufflo horn.

Directions　　Take it as drink, one dose daily.

Indications　　Chronic active hepatitis, hepatic cirrhosis at the initial stage. It can also be applied to prevent the occurrence of cirrhosis and even liver cancer.

Internal Diseases

SECTION 9 Constipation

Constipation refers to difficulty in defecation and prolonged interval between every two courses of defecation. It is responsible for prolonged retention of feces in the intestine. This long retention gets feces over-dried and hard to be discharged.

ETIOLOGY AND PATHOGENESIS

General excessive Yang and addiction to pungent and greasy food lead to accumulation of heat in the stomach and intestines; heat lingering after febrile disease consumes body fluid; deficiency of Qi and blood due to senile infirmity is responsible for dysfunction of the large intestine and scanty of body fluid; all the above are the causes of constipation.

MAIN SYMPTOMS AND SIGNS

1. Type of Excess: Dry feces, scanty and brown urine, flushed face, fever, or distending abdomen, dry mouth, restlessness, or frequent belching, fullness in the chest and hypochondria, poor appetite, reddened tongue with yellow,

dry coating, and slippery, rapid pulse.

2. Type of Deficiency: Constipation or smoothenless defecation, a little dry feces, defecating with effort followed by tiredness and even sweating and shortness of breath, pale complexion, lassitude, pale tongue with thin coating, weak pulse, or clear and abundant urine, cold limbs, cold pain of the loins and knees, or cold pain in the abdomen, etc..

Recipe 1

Ingredients

banana	250 g
crystal sugar	30 g

Process   Decoct all the ingredients in water.

Directions   Take the decoction, two doses daily for 5 days successively.

Indications   constipation.

Recipe 2

Ingredients

honey (*Mel*)	65 g
sesame oil	35 ml

Process   Add the sesame oil in the honey and infuse it with boiling water.

Directions   Take it twice daily, both in the morning and in the evening.

Indications   Constipation.

Internal Diseases

Recipe 3

Ingredients

Juda's ear	30 g
sea cucumber	30 g
pig's large intestine	150 g

salt, soya sauce, gourmet right amount for each

Process　Clean up the pig's large intestine and decoct it with other ingredients. When it is done, season it with condiments.

Directions　Eat the pig's large intestine and drink the soup.

Indications　Senile constipation due to deficiency of the blood and habitual constipation.

Recipe 4

Ingredients

　　bush-cherry seed (Semen Pruni)　　10 g
　　polished round-grained rice (Semen Oryzae Sativae)　　100 g
　　honey (Mel)　　right amount
　　ginger juice (Succus Zingiberis)　right amount

Process　Soak the bush-cherry seed in water, remove the its peel, and grind it into paste. Make a gruel with the rice, when it is nearly done, add in the paste, ginger juice and honey, go on cooking for a while.

Directions　Take it before meal.

Indications　Constipation.

Recipe 5

Ingredients

 milk　　　　　　　　　　　　　　　　250 g

 honey（*Mel*）　　　　　　　　　　　100 g

 scallion stalks（*Bulbus Allii Fistulosi*）　100 g

Process　Clean the scallion up, pound it in mash to get its juice, Heat the milk and honey in a pot, when it come to boil, add in the scallion juice and go on cooking for a while.

Directions　Take it before meal.

Indications　Senile habitual constipation and constipation due to the deficiency of yin and dryness of intestine.

Recipe 6

Ingredients

 honey（*Mel*）　　　　　　　　　　　6 g

 Chinese flowering quince（*Cydonia Lagenaria*）

 　　　　　　　　　　　　　　　　　　6 g

Process　Infuse the honey with the boiling water, and add in the powder of Chinese flowering quince.

Directions　Take it twice daily, both in the morning and in the evening.

Indications　Constipation and hematochezia.

Recipe 7

Ingredients

perilla seed (*Semen Perillae*)	15 g
white perilla seed	15 g
polished round-grained rice (*Semen Oryzae Sativae*)	30 g

Process　Wash perilla seed and white perilla seed clean and stir-fry them to dry. Pound them into paste and decoct in water. After it is done, filter it to get clear juice. Decoct the rice with juice to make gruel. Small amount of ginger juice and honey can be added as condiments.

Directions　Take the gruel frequently as tea.

Indications　Senile constipation with cough and dyspnea of qi deficiency type.

Recipe 8

Ingredients

Siberian solomonseal rhizome (*Rhizoma Polygonati*)	60 g
rehmannia root (*Radix Rehmanniae*)	60 g
honey (*Mel*)	right amount
egg	4

Process　Cut the rehmannia root and Siberian solomonseal rhizome into slices. Stew the eggs in water, when it is done, remove the shell of eggs. Decoct the first ingredients in water in a pot over a strong fire, when it come to boil, heat it over a slow fire for half an hour, let it cool and season it with honey before taking.

Directions Eat the eggs and drink the soup once daily.
Indications Constipation.

Recipe 9
Ingredients

sea cucumber	50 g
pig's large intestine	200 g
Juda's ear	20 g
millet wine	right amount
gourmet	right amount
powder of scallion and ginger, salt	right amount for each

Process Soak the sea cucumber in water and clean it up; clean the pig's large intestine up and spread right amount of salt over it to remove the dirty substance, cut it in sections. Put the pig's large intestine, sea cucumber and 木耳 in a pot, add in right amount of water, scallion, salt and millet wine, heat it over a strong fire, when it come to boil, heat it over a slow fire until it is well done, season it with gourmet.

Directions Take it with other foods.

Indications Constipation due to the dryness of the intestine.

Internal Diseases

Recipe 10

Ingredients

mulberry (*Fructus Mori*)   30 g

desertliving cistanche (*Herba Cistanchis*)
                                 15 – 30 g

sesame seed (*Semen Sesami Nigrum*)   15 g

parched fruit of citron (*Fructus Aurantii*)
                                 9 g

Process   Decoct all them in right amount of water and sift out the decoction from water.

Directions   Take it as drink once daily.

Indications   Constipation due to the deficiency of the yin and blood.

Recipe 11

Ingredients

lentinus (*Lentinus Edodes*)   500 g

fresh peach kernel (*Semen Persicae*)   200 g

chicken broth   550 g

salt, millet wine and sugar
                               right amount for each

Process   Peach kernel is steam until it is done. Add salt, millet, sugar in chicken broth and mix the mixture well. Decoct the mixture over fire until it comes to boils. Then add peach kernel and lentinus in the decoction and continue the decocting until it is done.

Directions Take it together with staple food.
Indications Constipation.

Recipe 12
Ingredients
  luffa (*Fructus Luffae*)   250 g
  lean pork   200 g
  slat right amount

Process Cut the luffa into cubes, the pork lean into slices, decoct the both ingredients in water, when it is done, season it with salt.

Directions Take it along with staple foods.
Indications Constipation.

Recipe 13
Ingredients
  parched apricot kernel (*Semen Armeniacae*)
                                            9 g
  pine nut   9 g
  hemp seed (*Fructus Cannabis*)   9 g
  arborvitae seed (*Semen Biotae*)   9 g

Process Pound all them into pieces, and infuse them with boiling water for a while.

Directions Take it as drink.

Indications Senile constipation or constipation due to deficiency of the yin.

SECTION 10 Malaria

Recipe 1
Ingredients
  fresh egg   1
  whitealcoholic drinks   20 ml
Process   Take the egg white and mix it with the spirit well.

Directions   Take it at once time, once weekly for 2 – 3 times.

Indications   Malaria.

Recipe 2
Ingredients
  soft – shelled turtle   1
  lard（*Lardum*）   20 g
  salt   right amount
Process   Kill the soft – shelled turtle and get rid of its entrails, cut it into cubes, put the meat and shell in a bowl, add in the lard, right amount of water and salt. Steam it over water in a steamer for 4 hours.

Directions　Eat the meat and drink the soup when it is hot.

Indications　Chronic malaria.

Recipe 3
Ingredients

mutton　　　　　　　　　　　　right amount
soft - shelled turtle (*Trioyx Sinensis*)
　　　　　　　　　　　　　　　　right amount
sugar　　　　　　　　　　　　　right amount
salt　　　　　　　　　　　　　　right amount

Process　Cut the mutton into dice, get rid of the entrails and head of soft - shelled turtle, decoct them with right amount of sugar and salt in water.

Directions　Eat the meat and drink a bowl of the soup daily.

Indications　malaria due to the deficiency of body and cold, or prolonged malaria.

Recipe 4
Ingredients

red phaseolus bean (*Semen Phaseoli*)　　100 g
red carp　　　　　　　　　　　　　　　　1
Chinese - date (*Fructus Ziziphi Jujubae*)　10
dried orange peel (*Pericarpium Citri*)　　5 g
ginger (*Zingiberis*)　　　　　　　　　　50 g

Process　Get rid of the scales and entrails of carp. decoct it with other ingredients in water.

Directions　Take it once a day.

Indications　Tertian fever, quartan malaria and prolonged malaria.

Recipe 5

Ingredients

　　sweet wormwood (*Herba Artemisiae*)　　50 g
　　peppermint (*Herba Menthae*)　　3 g

Process　Grind all them into raw powder, then infuse them with boiling water.

Directions　Take it as drink once daily.

Indications　Malaria.

SECTION 11 Hematochezia

Recipe 1
Ingredients
    oriental arborvitae twig   500 g
    polished round - grained rice (*Semen Oryzae Sativae*)   100 g
    brown sugar   right amount

Process   Cut oriental arborvitae twig into pieces, extract the juice of it. make a gruel with rice and right amount of water, when it is done, add in the juice of arborvitae twig and right amount of sugar.

Directions   Take it warmly.

Indications   Hematemesis, hematochezia, dysentery due to deficiency of spleen and heat evil in the stomach resulting in abnormal circulation of blood.

Recipe 2
Ingredients
    day lily (*Flos Hemerocallis*)   50 g
    Juda's ear   25 g

carbonized hair   10 g

Process   Decoct the first ingredients in 2 bowls of water until one bowl of decoction left, add in the carbonized hair in the bowl.

Directions   Take it along with the soup.

Indications   Hematochezia.

Recipe 3

Ingredients

dried tangerine (*Fructus Hordei*)   5
hawthorn fruit (*Fructus Crataegi*)   15 g
white sugar   9 g

Process   Decoct the three ingredients in water for 15 minutes.

Directions   Drink the decoction and eat the dregs.

Indications   Hematochezia.

Recipe 4

Ingredients

longan pulp (*Arillus Longan*)   150 g

Process   Put it in a bowl and steam it over water in a steamer.

Directions   Take it in twice daily.

Indications   arresting bleeding and removing the pain. It is applicable to hematochezia.

SECTION 12 Ascites

Recipe 1
Ingredients

    mutmeg (*Semen Myristicae*)   1.5 – 3 g
    polished round – grained rice (*Semen Oryzae Sativae*)   30 – 60 g
    ginger (*Zingiberis*)   2 slices

Process Heat the rice in water, when it have boiled for 10 minutes, add in the powder of the mutmeg and slices of ginger, go on cooking until it is done.

Directions Take it warmly and before the meal, once or twice daily.

Indications Distending pain in the gastric region, cold pain in the abdomen, scanty food – intake, nausea and vomiting.

Recipe 2
Ingredients

    soft – shelled turtle   1
    areca seed (*Semen Arecae*)   20 g

garlic 20 g

Process   Get rid of the head and entrails of the soft-shelled turtle and cut it into cubes, then decoct it with garlic and areca seed in water.

Directions   Eat the meal and drink the soup for 5 days.

Indications   Nourishing yin and dispersing retention. For liver cirrhosis with ascites.

Chapter One

SECTION 13 Hypertension

An elevated arterial pressure is probably the more important public health problem in developed countries − − being common, asymptomatic, readily detectable, usually easily treatable, and often leading to lethal complications if left untreated. Although our understanding of the pathophysiology of an elevated arterial pressure has increased, in 90 to 95 percent of cases the etiology (and thus potentially the prevention or cure)is still unknown.

DEFINITION

Since there is no dividing line between normal and high blood pressure but also systolic pressure, age, sex, and race. For example, patients with a diastolic pressure greater than 12.0 kPa (90 mmHg) will have a significant reduction in morbidity and mortality with adequate therapy. These , then, are patients who have hypertension and who should be considered for treatment.

The level of systolic pressure is important in assessing arterial pressures influence on cardiovascular morbidity . Males with normal diastolic pressures (< 10.9 kPa, 82 mmHg), but elevated systolic pressures (> 21 kPa, 158 mmHg) have a 2.5 fold increase in their cardiovascular mortality rates when compared with individuals with similar diastolic pressures but whose systolic pressures are normal (< 17.3 kPa, 130 mmHg).

Other significant factors which modify blood pressures influence on the frequency of morbid cardiovascular events are age, race, and sex with young black males being most adversely affected by hypertension.

Thus, even though in an adult hypertension is usually defined as a pressure greater than or equal to 20.0/12.0 kPa (150/90 mmHg), in men under 45 years of a pressure greater than or equal to 17.3/12.0 kPa (130/90 mmHg) may be elevated.

Individuals can be classified as being normotensive if arterial pressure is less than the levels noted above and as having destined hypertension if the diastolic pressure always exceeds these levels. Arterial pressure fluctuates in most persons, whether they are normotensive or hypertensive. Those who are classified as having labile hypertension are patients who sometimes but not always have arterial pressures within the hypertensive range. These patients are often considered to have borderline hypertension.

Sustained hypertension can become accelerated or enter malignant phase. Though a patient with malignant hypertension often has a blood pressure above 26.6/18.7 kPa (200/

140 mmHg), it is papilledema, usually accompanied by retinal hemorrhages and exudates, and not the absolute pressure level, that defines this condition. Accelerated hypertension signifies a significant recent increase over previous hypertensive levels associated with evidence of vascular damage on funduscopic examination but without papilledema.

In 1978, World Health Organization (WHO) determined;

1. Normal blood pressure: Systolic pressure$\leqslant$18.7Kpa (140 mmHg), diastolic$\leqslant$12.0 kPa (90 mmHg). 2. Hypertension: Systolic pressure$\geqslant$21.3 kPa(160 mmHg) or diastolic pressure$\geqslant$12.6 kPa (95 mmHg). 3. Borderline hypertension: Systolic pressure 18.9 ~ 21.1 kPa (141 ~ 159 mmHg), diastolic pressure 12.1 ~ 12.5 kPa (91 ~ 94 mmHg). ETIOLOGY

The cause of elevated arterial pressure is unknown in most cases. There are no available data to define the frequency of secondary hypertension in the general population, although in middle – – aged males it has been reported to be 6 percent. On the other hand, in referral centers where patients undergo an extensive evaluation, it has been reported to be as high as 35 percent.

ESSENTIAL HYPERTENSION Patients with arterial hypertension and no definable cause are said to have primary, essential, or idiopathic hypertension. By definition, the underlying mechanism(s) is unknown; however, the kidney probably plays a central role.

1. Heredity   Genetic factors have long been assumed to be important in the genesis of hypertension . One approach has been to assess the correlation of blood pressures within familial aggregation). From these studies the minimum size of the genetic factor can be expressed by a correlation coefficient of approximately 0.2.

2. Environment   A number of environmental factors have been specifically implicated in the development of hypertension including salt intake, obesity, occupation, family size, and crowding. These factors have all been assumed to be important in the increase in blood pressure with age in more affluent societies , in contrast to the decline in blood pressure with age in more primitive cultures. Indeed, even the familial aggregation of blood pressure has been suggested as being related, at least in part, to environmental rather than genetic factors. However, since adopted children do not demonstrate familial aggregation of blood pressure, this phenomenon is probably almost entirely the result of genetic factors.

3. Factors modifying the course of essential hypertension   Age, race, sex, smoking, serum cholesterol, glucose intolerance, weight, and perhaps renin activity may all alter the prognosis of this disease.

SECONDARY HYPERTENSION   In only a small minority of patients with an elevated arterial pressure can a specific cause be identified. Nearly all the secondary forms are related to an alteration in hormone secretion and /or renal function.

1. Renal hypertension   Hypertension produced by renal disease is the result of either (1) a derangement in the renal handling of sodium and fluids leading to volume expansion or (2) an alteration in renal secretion of vasoactive materials resulting in a systemic or local change in arteriolar tone. A simple explanation for renal vascular hypertension is that decreased perfusion of renal tissue due to stenosis of a main or branch renal artery activates the vasoconstriction, by stimulation of aldosterone secretion with resultant sodium retention, and/or by stimulating the adrenergic nervous system. In actual practice only about one – half of patients with renovascular hypertension have elevated absolute levels of renin activity in peripheral plasma , although when renin measurements are referenced against an index of sodium balance, a much higher fraction has inappropriately high values.

A recently described form of renal hypertension results from the excess secretion of renin by juxtaglomerular cell tumors or nephroblastomas. The initial presentation has been similar to that of hyperaldosteronism with hypertension , hypokalemia, and overproduction of aldosterone. However, on contrast to primary aldosteronism, peripheral renal activity is elevated instead of subnormal. This disease can be distinguished from other form of secondary aldosteronism by the presence of normal renal function and with unilateral increases internal vein renin concentration without a renal artery lesion.

2. Endocrine hypertension (adrenal hypertension)

Hypertension is a feature of a variety of adrenal cortical abnormalities. In primary aldosteronism there is a clear relationship between the aldosterone – induced, sodium retention and the hypertension. Normal individuals given aldosterone develop hypertension only if they also ingest sodium. Since aldosterone causes sodium retention by stimulating renal tubular exchange of sodium for potassium, hypokalemia is a prominent feature in mist patients with primary aldosteronism, and the measurement of serum potassium provides a simple screening test, The effect of sodium retention and volume expansion in chronically suppressing plasma renin activity is critically important for the definitive diagnosis. In most clinical situations plasma renin activity and plasma or urinary aldosterone levels parallel each other, but on patients with primary aldosteronism, aldosterone levels are high and relatively fixed because of autonomous aldosterone secretion, while plasma renin activity levels are suppressed and respond sluggishly to sodium deletion. Primary aldosteronism may be secondary either to a tumor or bilateral adrenal hyperplasia. It is important to distinguish between these two conditions preoperatively, as usually the hypertension in the latter is not modified by operation.

The most common cause of endocrine hypertension is that resulting from the use of estrogen-containing oral contraceptives. Indeed, this may be the most common form of secondary hypertension. The mechanism producing the hypertension is likely to be secondary to activation of the renin-angiotensin-aldosterone system.

3. Coarctation of the aorta The hypertension associated with coarctation may be caused by the constriction itself, or perhaps by the changes in the renal circulation which result in an unusual form of renal arterial hypertension. The diagnosis of coarctation is usually evident from physical examination and routine x-ray findings.

4. Low-renin essential hypertension Approximately 20 percent of patients who by all other criteria have essential hypertension have suppressed plasma renin activity. Recent studies have suggested that many of these patients have an increased sensitivity to angiotensin 2 which may be the underlying mechanism: Since this altered sensitivity has been reported even in patients with normal renin hypertension, it is likely that patients with low-renin hypertension are not a distinct subset but rather form part of a continuum of patients with essential hypertension.

5. High-renin essential hypertension Approximately 15 percent of patients with essential hypertension have plasma renin levels elevated above the normal range. It has been suggested that plasma renin plays an important role in the

pathogenesis of the elevated blood pressure in these patients. However, most studies have documented that saralasin significantly reduces blood pressure in less than half of these patients. This has led some investigators to postulate that the elevated renin levels and blood pressure may both be secondary to an increased activity of the adrenergic system. It has been proposed that, in those patients with angiotensin-dependent high-renin hypertension whose arterial pressures are lowered by saralasin, the mechanism responsible for the increased renin and, therefore, the hypertension is a compensatory hyperreninemia secondary to a decreased adrenal responsiveness to angiotensin II.

EFFECTS OF HYPERTENSION

For nearly 70 years it has been known that patients with hypertension die prematurely. The most common cause of death is heart disease, with strokes and renal failure also frequently occurring, particularly in those with significant retinopathy.

EFFECTS ON HEART   Cardiac compensation for the excessive work load imposed by increased systemic pressure is at first sustained by left ventricular hypertrophy. Ultimately, the function of this chamber deteriorates, it dilates, and the symptoms and signs of heart failure appear. Angina pectoris may also occur because of accelerated coronary arterial disease and /or increased myocardial oxygen requirements as a consequence of the increased myocardial mass, which exceeds the capacity of the coronary circulation. On physical examination the heart is enlarged and has a prominent left ventricular impulse. The sound of aortic closure is accentuated, and there may be a faint murmur of aortic regurgitation. Presystolic (atrial, fourth) heart sounds appear frequently on hypertensive heart disease, and a protodiastolic (ventricular, third heart) sound or summation gallop rhythm may be present. Electrocardiographic changes of left ventricular hypertrophy are common; evidence of ischemia or infarction may be observed late in the disease. The majority of deaths due to hypertension result from myocardial infarction or congestive heart failure.

NEUROLOGIC EFFECTS   The neurologic effects of long-standing hypertension may be divided into retinal and central nervous system changes. Because the retina is the only tissue in which the arteries and arterioles can be examined directly, repeated ophthalmoscopic examination provides the opportunity to observe the progress of the vascular effects of hypertension. The Keith-Wagener-Barker classification of the retinal changes in hypertension has provided a simple and excellent means for serial evaluation of the hypertensive patient. Increasing severity of hypertension is associated with focal spasm and progressive general narrowing of the arterioles, as well as the appearance of hemorrhages, exudates, and papilledema. These retinal lesions often produce scotomata, blurred vision and even blindness especially in the presence of papilledema or hemorrhages of the macular area. Hypertensive lesions may develop acutely and if therapy results in significant reduction of blood pressure, may show rapid resolution. Rarely, these lesions resolve without therapy. In contrast, retinal arteriolosclerosis results from endothelial and muscular proliferation, and it accurately reflects similar changes in other organs. Sclerotic changes do not develop as rapidly as hypertensive lesions, nor do they regress appreciably with therapy. As a consequence of increased wall thickness and rigidity, sclerotic arterioles distort and compress the veins as they cross within their common fibrous sheath, and the reflected light streak from the arterioles is changed by the increased opacity of the vessel wall.

Central nervous system dysfunction also occurs frequently in patients with hypertension. Occipital headaches . most often in the morning, are among the most prominent early symptoms of hypertension. Dizziness, light - headedness, vertigo, tinnitus, and dimmed vision or syncope may also be observed, but the more serious manifestations are due to vascular occlusion or hemorrhage.

RENAL EFFECTS Arteriolosclerotic lesions of the afferent and efferent arterioles and the glomerular capillary tufts are the most common renal vascular lesions in hypertension and result in decreased glomerular filtration rate and tubular dysfunction. Proteinuria and microscopic hematuria occur because of glomerular lesions , and approximately 10 percent of the deaths secondary to hypertension result from renal failure, Blood loss in hypertension occurs not only from renal lesions; epistaxis, hemoptysis, and metrorrhagia also occur most frequently in these patients.

In general, traditional Chinese treatment of hypertension lowers the blood pressure less but relieves hypertensive symptoms better than western medicines. Therefore, combined TCM and Western medicine is a logical approach for hypertension.

MAIN POINTS OF PATHOGENESIS

Hypertension is included in the categories of "xuan yun" (vertigo) and "tou tong" (headache). It is common thought that hypertension occurs when incoordination between yin and yang is caused by impairment of seven modes of emotion, improper diet, internal damage and deficiency. The main injured viscera are heart, liver and kidney.

1. Hyperactivity of liver - yang: It is usually postulated that long - term emotional, upsets or grief easily lead to stagnation of the liver - energy with formation of evil fire, manifesting as headache, dizziness, tinnitus, restlessness, flushed face and others. Overexertion or body debility and general hypofunction may induce consumption of blood or deficiency of yin and gradually leads to the inequality of yin and yang in which the yin is unable to inhibit yang - energy and over - activity of yang ensues, and in turn, the hyperactivity of yang may further consumes the yin - fluid which further

results in development of liver yang hyperactivity due to deficiency of yin - fluid. Sthenia of liver - yang usually occurs in mild hypertension.

2. Deficiency of the liver - yin and kidney - yin: Liver and kidney is said to come from the same origin. Between them there are the mutual supply of nutrients and the close relationship. Liver stores blood and kidney stores essence. The blood and essence are able to transform each other. Insufficiency of kidney - yin usually causes insufficiency of liver - yin and vice versa, which would lead to the deficiency of the liver - yin and kidney - yin. It usually presents in some of patients with hypertension and probably accounts for the hypertension in these patients.

3. Deficiency of yin leading to hyperactivity of yang: It is a morbid condition due to the consumption of essence, blood and body fluid, which can lead to the inequality of yin and yang, in which the yin is unable to inhibit yang - energy and over - activity of yang ensues, and, in turn, the hyperactivity of yang may further consumes the yin - fluid. In clinic, the diagnosis may be established by concomitant appearance of the deficiency of liver - yin and kidney - yin accompanying with sthenia of liver - yang.

4. Deficiency of heart - yin: Heart - yin is the nutritious fluid of the heart and a component of blood. It has a close relation to the heart - blood physiologically and pathologically, and also to the condition of lung - yin and kidney -

yin. Deficiency of kidney - yin may cause that water fails to inhibit fire which will gradually lead to an excess of fire and eventually result in the deficiency of heart - yin. The common features, such as palpitation, insomnia, dreaminess and amnesia, are sought in most of the patients with hypertension.

5. Deficiency of both yin and yang : It is a morbid condition characterized by simultaneously occurrence of deficiency of yin and yang and usually seen in the later stage of hypertension. The cause is that yang is involved by deficient yin such as kidney damage resulting in chronic renal failure. This type is less than another types in hypertension patients.

6. Deficiency of both vital energy and yin: It is a morbid condition of damage of both yin fluid and yang energy occurring in the course of hypertension in moderate depth. Vital energy is the functions of various organs and tissues of the body, which is included in the categories of yang in traditional Chinese medicine. Deficiency of vita energy may cause hypofunction of viscera and lowering of metabolism due to insufficiency of yang - energy with failure to warm and nourish the viscera, manifesting as pale complexion, dizziness, tinnitus, palpitation, shortness of breath, lassitude and spontaneous sweating. deficiency of yin may cause hyperactivity of fire, manifesting as hot feeling of the palms and soles , red lips , dry mouth, oliguria with yellowish urine, constipation, red and uncoated tongue, headache and others. In an indi-

vidual patient when there are simultaneously some of the symptoms of both efficiency of vital energy and deficiency of yin, the diagnosis of this type may be established by carefully examination.

7. Maladjustment of chong and ren channels: It may result from impairment of the liver and kidney, elderly and climacteric irregular menstruation and is usually seen in the female patients with hypertension. Irregular menstruation usually occurs preceding the amenorrhea. In the menstrual period, there are obviously fluctuation of the blood pressure and general malaise, which easily induce to elevate the level of the blood pressure.

Recipe 1

Ingredients

black bone chicken	100 – 200 g
cordyceps (*Cordyceps*)	10 g
Chinese yam (*Rhizoma Dioscoreae*)	30 g

Process Kill the black bone chicken and get rid of the feather and entrails, clean it up and cut in into cubes, decoct it with other ingredients in right amount of water over a slow fire, when it come to boil, go on heat it over a slow fire until the meat is well done.

Directions Eat the meat and drink the soup.

Indications Diabetes, hypertension, hectic fever and

night sweat.

Recipe 2

Ingredients

    tremella (*tremella*)   20 g

    prepared eucommia bark (*Cortex Eucommiae Praeparata*)   20 g

    lucid ganoderma (*Ganoderma Lucidum*)   10 g

    crystal sugar   150 g

Process Clean the eucommia bark and lucid ganoderma up and decoct them with water for three times, then put all the decoctions together and decoct it until there is 1000 ml left. Soak the tremella in water, clean it up, add right amount of water in it and decoct it over a slow fire until it becomes yellowish, then add in the thick decoction of eucommia and lucid ganoderma and go on decoct it over a slow fire to make gruel, add in the sugar and have it dissolved.

Directions Take it twice daily, both in the morning and in the evening respectively, one bowl each time.

Indications Nourishing the yin and moistening the lung, replenishing the stomach and prompting the production of bodily fluid. It is applicable to hypertension due to deficiency of both kidney and spleen, with headache, tinnitus, insomnia and lassitude in the loin and legs.

Internal Diseases

Recipe 3

Ingredients

 water chestnut (*Bulbus Heleocharis Tuberosae*)
                 100 g

 jellyfish   100 g

Process Decoct the two ingredients in right amount of water.

Directions Take it twice daily, once in the morning and once in the evening respectively.

Indications Hypertension.

Recipe 4

Ingredients

 gastrodia tuber (*Rhizoma Gastrodiae*) 10 g
 pig's brain   1
 polished round-grained rice (*Semen Oryzae Sativae*)   250 g

Process Decoct all them in right amount of water to make gruel.

Directions Take it warmly in every morning.

Indications Hypertension and arteriosclerosis, Ménière's disease, and hemiparalysis due to cerebrovascular accident, etc..

Recipe 5

Ingredients

glehnia root (*Radix Glehniae*) 20 g
ophiopogon root (*Radix Ophiopogonis*) 20 g
fresh pueraria root (*Radix Puerariae*) 10 g
round – polished glutinous rice (*Semen Oryzae Sativae*) 60 g

Process   Decoct all them in right amount of water in an earthenware pot to make them into gruel.

Directions   Take the gruel along with meals.

Indications   Hypertension due to deficiency of both yin and yang.

Recipe 6

Ingredients

fleece – flower root (*Radix Polygoni Multiflori*) 60 g
polished round – grained rice (*Semen Oryzae Sativae*) 100 g
Chinese – date (*Fructus Ziziphi Jujubae*) 3
crystal sugar   right amount

Process   Decoct the fleece – flower root in water, sift out the decoction from dregs, Decoct other ingredients in the filtrate to make gruel.

Directions   Take the gruel along with meals.

Indications   Invigorate the kidney and liver. For hypertension due to deficiency of liver and kidney.

Recipe 7

Ingredients

    hawthorn fruit（*Fructus Crataegi*） 30 – 40 g

    polished round – grained rice（*Semen Oryzae Sativae*） 100 g

    granulated sugar 10 g

Process Decoct the hawthorn in right amount of water, sift out the thick decoction from dregs, add in the rice and crystal sugar and go on cooking to make a gruel.

Directions Take it once in the morning and once in the morning respectively, together with staple food. Taking the gruel on an empty stomach prohibited. One course consists of 7 – 10 days.

Indications Invigorate the spleen and stomach, eliminate dyspepsia, remove blood stasis. For indigestion, diarrhea, abdominal pain, postpartum tormina, lochiorrhea, delayed menstruation, dysmenorrhea, infantile indigestion, hypertension, coronary heart disease, and hyperlipemia. Contraindicated for cases of chronic deficiency of the spleen and stomach type.

Recipe 8

Ingredients

    prunella spike（*Spica Prunellae*） 20 g

    lean pork 50 g

Process Cut the lean into slices, then decoct it and

prunella spike in right amount of water to make soup.

Directions Eat the meat and drink the soup twice daily.

Indications Hypertension, low - grade fever in cases with pulmonary tuberculosis. A long - term treatment should be given.

Recipe 9

Ingredients

soaked sea cucumber	50 g
crystal sugar	right amount

Process Decoct the sea cucumber in water, when it is well done, add in the crystal sugar and go on cooking for a while to make soup.

Directions Take it on an empty stomach before breakfast.

Indications Invigorate the kidney and enhance vital essence, moisturize dryness by nourishing blood. For hypertension.

Recipe 10

Ingredients

pig's bile (*Fel Suilum*)	200 g
mung bean (*Semen Phaseoli Radiati*)	100 g

Process Mix the flour of the mung bean in the pig's bile, then dry it under the sun, grind it into fine powder.

Internal Diseases

Directions   Take it 10 g each time, twice daily.

Indications   Clear away heat and calm the liver. For hypertension.

Chapter One

SECTION 14　Coronary Heart Disease

Coronary atherosclerotic heart disease, known as "coronary heart disease"(CHD), or "ischemic heart disease". It refers to the heart disease induce by myocardial ischemia, and oxygen deficit caused by coronary atherosclerosis. The incidence is high in all the countries especially in the developed countries. Recently, the incidence in China is increasing.

In most western countries, angiocardiopathy is the first among the list of causes of death, Covering half of total mortality, more than half of which is caused by coronary artery disease. For instance, over 600 thousands out of 20 billions people in the United States die from CAD every year. According to the analysis records of postmortem examination, the same degree of atherosclerosis of coronary artery in our country is $15-20$ years later than that in western countries. Latent coronary artery disease covers $70-90\%$ of coronary artery disease found in our country. In 1972, a general cheek - up was carried out among 3474 residents over 40 years old in Shijiazhuang district. The number of the people who were found to suffer from coronary artery disease was 233, 6.71% of the all residents in the district. Of all the cases, 79.4% pertained to latent coronary artery disease. Because of the different locations, extents and degrees of the coronary lesion, and different clinical characteristics, according to the diagnostic criteria made by WHO, coronary heart disease can be divided into: (1) primary sudden cardiac arrest; (2) angina pectoris; (3) myocardiac infarction; (4) heart failure due to coronary heart disease and (5) arrhythmia. This disease, in TCM, pertains to the categories of "xiong bi" (obstruction of qi in the chest), "xiong tong" (precordial pain with cold limbs). The mild case is named as "jue xin tong", "pectoral pains"; the serious case is named as "zhen xin tong", "true heartache". Ben Xu means deficiency of the fundamental, biaoshi means excess of the incidental, deficiency includes yin, yang, qi and blood, phlegm, blood stasis, fire and stagnancy belong to 'excess'. This disease is located at the heart but is related to the spleen and the kidney. Its general mechanism is deficiency in the fundamental aspect of the body and excessiveness in the external symptoms. The fundamental aspect and external symptoms, deficiency and excess should be distinguished when we differentiate types based on symptom – signs. But in clinical practice, deficiency and excessiveness are often seen at the same time. Thus doctors should consider the serious extent of deficiency and excessiveness to decide their clinical treatment. The risk factors for coronary heart disease are hypertension, hyperlipemia, diabetes mellitus and cigarette-smoking..

DIAGNOSIS

1. Angina Pectoris

Angina pectoris is caused by transient myocardial ischemia due to decreased coronary flow, manifested as episodic retrosternal pain, smothering and choking, etc.

1) Overworked angina: A transient attack of chest pain is induced by exertion, heavy meals, exposure to cold, or emotion. The typical manifestations are sudden attacks of retrosternal constricting oppressive pain or gripping pain. The pain commonly radiates to the left shoulder and left arm, accompanied with cold sweat. The pain lasts 1 - 5 minutes and can be relieved by resting or by placing a nitroglycerin tablet under the tongue. Overworked angina can be divided into incipient type, stable type and increscent type. In incipient type the duration of the illness is within one month. In stable type, the state of illness can be stable for a long time. The episodes have a definite regularity. In increscent type both the incidence and the severity of the attack increase, indicating the unstableness of the disease.

2) Spontaneous angina: The episodes are not related to exertion. The attack may occur in the recumbent position or during sleep, accompanied with restlessness, fright and hy-

pertension. The symptoms persist longer and become more severe which could not be relieved by nitroglycerin.

Variant angina is a special type of angina pectoris. It is considered that the attacks are related to the spasm of the major one of coronary arteries. Its symptoms are similar to hose of spontaneous angina. Many attacks may occur cyclically in a day. During the episodes ECG shows ST - segment elevation.

In incipient angina, increscent angina, spontaneous angina and variant angina, the state of illness changes rapidly and transforms in a short period. This is a transitional state. Therefore, they are also called unstable angina and patients need to be admitted for treatment.

3) Electrocardiographic examination is convenient for the diagnosis of angina pectoris. During the attack of angina, most cases show various degrees of T wave or accompanied with different types of arrhythmia. In the cases of variant angina and some spontaneous angina, ST segment elevation may be present, suggesting transmural ischemia at corresponding walls of ventricle. To exercise electrocardiogram stress test can help physicians in confirming the diagnosis of untypical cases.

4) Coronary arteriography is an invasive procedure by which the disease status and left ventricle function of more than 90% of the patients with coronary heart disease can give us some parameters for reference but its value in the di-

agnosis of coronary heart disease is limited. Radionuclide scanning is very helpful in diagnosing ischemic heart disease and evaluating heart function.

2. Myocardiac Infarction

Myocardiac infarction is the myocardial necrosis resulting from persistent and severe myocardial ischemia due to occlusion of a coronary artery and interruption of myocardial blood supply. Myocardiac infarction can be complicated by arrhythmia, heart failure, and cardiogenic shock. In severe cases or in patients who are not treated in time, death usually ensues.

1) Premonitory symptoms of myocardiac infarction: Some patients may have premonitory symptoms for a period of time prior to the onset of myocardiac infarction. The patients may have frequent episodes of angina pectoris which last longer and more severe or are accompanied with nausea, vomiting and arrhythmia. The episodes can not be relieved by placing nitroglycerin tablet under the tongue. But many patients have not premonitory symptoms prior to the episode.

2) Clinical manifestations of myocardiac infarction: Retrosternal or precordial persistent pain occurs suddenly with a sensation of oppression. The pain may radiate to the neck and left shoulder. The patients commonly have profuse sweating, anxiety, pallor, thready pulse and lowering of blood pressure. In some of senile patients, the pain may not

be obvious but confusional state, shock and heart failure are commonly seen.

3) In acute myocardiac infarction the electrocardiogram shows specific changes. In acute stage all the leads relevant to the site of infarction show arcuate elevation of ST segments, inversion of T waves and appearance of pathologic Q waves. Subsequently, as the disease turns better, the electrocardiogram undergoes a stereotyped changes.

4) Serum enzyme studies are very valuable for the diagnosis of acute myocardiac infarction. Their accuracies are high. Creatinine phosphokinase (CPK) and the MB isoenzyme are very valuable for diagnosing early myocardiac infarction. Serum glutamic oxalacetic transaminase (SGOT), lactic dehydrogenase (LDH) and isoenzymes are of value in the diagnosis of myocardiac infarction. In addition, the examinations of leukocyte count, blood sugar and serum myoglobin are also helpful for the diagnosis and the prognosis of the disease.

Recipe 1

Ingredients

fleece − flower root (*Radix Polygoni Multiflori*)
50 g
black soybean (*Semen Sojae Nigrum*) 50 g
flesh of pangolin (*Manis Pentadactyla*) 250 g

salt   right amount

Process Cut the pangolin into pieces, clean the fleece-flower root and black soybean up, decoct them in 500 ml of water over a slow fire for 90 minutes, when the black soybean is well done, season it with gourmet.

Directions Eat the meat and bean, drink the soup.

Indications coronary heart disease, hypertension, and hyperlipemia.

Recipe 2

Ingredients

    mung bean（*Semen Phaseoli Radiati*）

                                       right amount

    polished round-grained rice（*Semen Oryzae Sativae*）

                                       right amount

Process Soak the mung bean in warm water for 2 hours, then decoct it with rice in 1000 ml of water until the mung bean is well done and getting a thick gruel.

Directions Take it twice or three times daily.

Indications Coronary heart disease and summer heat.

Recipe 3

Ingredients

black edible fungus（*Auricularia*）	6 g
lean pork	50 g

finger of citron (*Fructus Citri Sarcodactulis*)
9 g

coix seed (*Semen Coicis*) 20 g

Process   Decoct all them in water.
Directions   Take it one dose daily.
Indications   Coronary heart disease.

Recipe 4
Ingredients

ginseng powder (*Pulvis Radix Ginseng*)   3 g
polished round - grained rice (*Semen Oryzae Sativae*)   60 g
sugar   right amount

Process   Decoct all the ingredients in water to make a gruel.

Directions   Take it as breakfast, one dose daily.
Indications   Coronary heart disease.

Recipe 5
Ingredients

sea cucumber   50 g
Chinese - date (*Fructus Ziziphi Jujubae*)   5
crystal sugar   right amount

Process   Decoct the sea cucumber in right amount of water until it is well done, add in the Chinese - date and crystal sugar and go on cooking for 15 - 20 minutes.

Directions　Take it as breakfast.

Indications　Coronary heart disease.

Recipe 6

Ingredients

ginseng (*Radix Ginseng*)	20 g
notoginseng (*Radix Notoginseng*)	20 g
amber (*Succini*)	10 g

Process　Grind all them into fine powder.

Directions　Take it three times daily, 0.6 g for each time.

Indications　Coronary heart disease.

Recipe 7

Ingredients

chrysanthemum flower (*Flos Chrysanthemi*)	5 g
raw hawthorn fruit (*Fructus Crataegi*)	10 g
cassia seed (*Semen Cassiae*)	15 g

Process　Decoct all them in water in an earthenware pot for 20 minutes.

Directions　Take the decoction in any time.

Indications　Coronary heart disease and hypertension.

Recipe 8

Ingredients

      red sage root（*Radix Salviae Miltiorrhizae*）
                                                    10 g
      slices of Chinese hawthorn（*Fructus Crataegi*）
                                                    10 g
      ophiopogon root（*Radix Ophiopogonis*） 5 g

Process   Infuse all them with boiling water, seal the container for 30 minutes.

Directions   Take it warmly.

Indications   Coronary heart disease and hypertension.

Recipe 9

Ingredients

    honey（*Mel*）   25 g
    fleece - flower root（*Radix Polygoni Multiflori*）
                                                25 g
    red sage root（*Radix Salviae Miltiorrhizae*）
                                                25 g

Process   Decoct the fleece - flower root and red sage seed in water, sift out the decoction from dregs, then add in the honey.

Directions   Take it one dose daily.

Indications   Coronary heart disease, coronary arteriosclerosis, liver diseases.

Recipe 10

Ingredients

ginkgo leaf (*Folium Ginkgo*) 15 g
trichosanthes fruit (*Fructus Trichosanthis*)
 15 g
red sage root (*Radix Salviae Miltiorrhizae*)
 15 g
macrostem onion (*Bulbus Allii Macrostemi*)
 12 g
curcuma root (*Radix Curcumae*) 10 g
liquorice (*Radix Glycyrrhizae*) 4.5 g

Process   Decoct all them in water.

Directions   Take the decoction both in the morning and in the evening.

Indications   Coronary heart disease.

SECTION 15 Hyperthyroidism

Recipe 1
Ingredients
  astragalus root (*Radix astragali seu Hedysari*)
  45 g
  rehmannia root (*Radix Rehmanniae*) 12 g
  white peony root (*Radix Paeoniae Alba*)
  12 g
  cyperus tuber (*Rhizoma Cyperi*) 12 g
  prunella spike (*Spica Prunellae*) 30 g
  fleece − flower root (*Radix Polygoni Multiflori*)
  20 g

Process Decoct them in right amount of water.
Directions Take it in twice daily, one dose daily. One course consists of half or one year.
Indications Hyperthyroidism.

Recipe 2
Ingredients
  poria (*Poria*) 60 g

    oriental water plantain rhizome (*Rhizoma Alismatis*)   20 g
    peel of areca seed (*Pericarpium Arecae*) 20 g
    astragalus root (*Radix astragali seu Hedysari*)
                                                       20 g
    red peony root (*Radix Paeoniae Rubra*) 20 g
    red sage root (*Radix Salviae Miltiorrhizae*)
                                                       20 g
    cinnamon twig (*Ramulus Cinnamomi*)   15 g
    ginger (*Rhizoma Zingiberis*)   15 g
    Trichosanthes Palmata   15 g
    Chinese - date (*Fructus Ziziphi Jujubae*)
                                                       15 g

Process   Decoct all them in right amount of water.
Directions   Take it in twice and one dose daily.
Indications   Hyperthyroidism.

Recipe 3
Ingredients
    day lily (*Flos Hemerocallis*)   30 g
    portulaca (*Herba Portulacae*)   30 g
Process   Decoct them in right amount of water.
Directions   Take it when one is thirst.
Indications   Hyperthyroidism with irritability, flush, bitter taste, dizziness, yellow tongue fur, etc..

Recipe 4

Ingredients

sea cucumber	300 g
lentinus (*Lentinus Edodes*)	200 g
lean pork	600 g
powder of soybean	
white sugar	
egg	
salt	
edible oil	right amount

Process Chop lean pork up and put the meat stuffing in a bowl, add right amount of bean flour, white sugar, salt, sesame oil, and eggs, mix the mixture well. Then the mixture is divided into three portions. Stir − fry the pork stuffing wrapped with dry bean flour in edible oil until the surface becomes brown. Then stir − fry sea cucumber and lentinus in edible oil over a slow fire for a few seconds, then add in stir − fried pork stuffing and stew the mixture until it is done.

Directions Take 50 − 100 g each time, twice daily.

Indications Hyperthyroidism with irritability and insomnia, palpitation, profuse sweat, dizziness, feverish sensation in the palms and soles, swelling of the neck, etc..

SECTION 16 Simple Obesity

Recipe 1
Ingredients
> *red phaseolus bean* (*Semen Phaseoli*)   50 g
> *tangerine peel* (*Pericarpium Citri Reticulatae*)
> 6 g
> *carp*   1 (about 1000 g)

Process Get rid of the scales and entrails of the carp, then put the other ingredients in the cave of the carp, put it in a big bowl and add in right amount of water and other condiments, steam it over water in a steamer.

Directions Eat the fish and drink the soup.
Indications Simple obesity.

Recipe 2
Ingredients
> *milk*   100 ml
> *tea leaves* (*Thea*)   3 g
> *white sugar*   right amount

Process P it the tea in a cup, infuse it with boiling water for later use. Heat the milk in a pot, then add in the sugar and the tincture.

Directions   Take it as drink.

Indications   Simple obesity, diabetes, appetite, poor indigestion., constipation.

Recipe 3

Ingredients

 tea   3 g

 pod of Chinese scholartree（Fructus Sophorae）

                18 g

 fleece - flower root（Radix Polygoni Multiflori）

                30 g

 waxgourd peel（Exocarpium Benincasae）

                18 g

 hawthorn fruit（Fructus Crataegi）   15 g

Process   decoct the first four ingredients in boiling water for 20 minutes, then infuse the tea with the boiling decoction.

Directions   Take it as drink, one dose daily.

Indications   Simple obesity.

SECTION 17 Insolation

Recipe 1
Ingredients
    Hindu lotus petiole   30 g
    willow leaf   6 g
    pueraria root (*Radix Puerariae*)   6 g
    hyacinth bean (*Semen Dolichoris*)   15 g

Process   Decoct them in 3 bowls of water over a slow fire until one bowl of decoction left.

Directions   Take it at once time, two dose daily.

Indications   Insolation.

Recipe 2
Ingredients
    white hyacinth bean (*Semen Dolichoris*) 50 g
    crystal sugar   30 g
    round - polished glutinous rice (*Semen Oryzae Sativae*)   50 g
    fresh lotus leaf (*Folium Nelumbinis*)   1

Process   Decoct the white hyacinth bean in right

amount of water, when it come to boil, add in the rice and go on cooking it over a slow fire. When the white hyacinth bean is become soft, add in the crystal sugar and lotus leaf, go on cooking for 20 minutes.

Directions　Take it at once times, two doses daily for 3 days successively.

Indications　Insolation.

Recipe 3

Ingredients

　　fresh agastache (*Herba Pogostemonis seu Agastachis*)　　　　　　　　　　　　　　　6 g
　　fresh eupatorium (*Herba Eupatorii*)　6 g
　　fresh lotus leaf (*Folium Nelumbinis*)　6 g
　　fresh rehmannia root (*Radix Rehmanniae*)
　　　　　　　　　　　　　　　　　　6 g
　　fresh fleece – flower root (*Radix Polygoni Multiflori*)　　　　　　　　　　　　　　　5 g
　　fresh pear (*Succus Piri*) *juice*　　10 g
　　white sugar　　　　　　　　right amount

Process　Chop the above ingredients to get juice. Decoct the juice with a right amount of water over fire until 15 minutes after it comes to boil. Add sugar, etc. and mix the drink well.

Directions　Take the drink frequently.

Indications　Insolation with thirst, restlessness, palpitation, dizziness, etc..

Recipe 4
Ingredients

isatis leaf (*Folium Isatidis*)	30 – 60 g
honeysuckle flower (*Flos Lonicerae*)	15 g
tea leaves (*Thea*)	5 g

Process　decoct all them in right amount of water or infuse it with boiling water for 20 minutes,

Directions　Take it as drink, one dose daily.

Indications　Insolation.

Recipe 5
Ingredients

peppermint (*Herba Menthae*)	4 g
elscholtzia (*Herba Elsholtzae*)	3 g
lophatherum (*Herba Lophatheri*)	3 g
plantain herb (*Herba Plantaginis*)	5 g

Process　Decoct the last three ingredients in right amount of water in an earthenware pot for 5 minutes, add in the peppermint and go on cooking for another five minutes.

Directions　Take it one dose daily.

Indications　Insolation.

SECTION 18 Simple Goiter

Recipe 1
Ingredients
    curcuma root (*Radix Curcumae*)   9 g
    red sage root (*Radix Salviae Miltiorrhizae*)
                                              15 g
    seaweed (*Sargassum*)   15 g
    brown sugar   right amount

Process   Decoct the first ingredients in right amount of water, sift out the decoction from dregs, season it with brown sugar.

Directions   Take it one dose daily for 4 weeks successively.

Indications   Simple goiter.

Recipe 2
Ingredients
    white radish (*Napus*)   250 g
    laver   15 g
    dried orange peel (*Pericarpium Citri*)   2 g

salt, vinegar　　　　　　　right amount for each

Process　Clean the white radish up and cut it into threads, then tear up the laver and dried orange peel, decoct them in right amount of water over a slow fire for half an hour, then season it with salt, vinegar and gourmet.

Directions　Drink the soup and one dose daily.

Indications　Simple goiter.

Recipe 3
Ingredients

kelp (*Thallus Laminariae*)	120 g
vinegar	1000 g
citron fruit (*Fructus Citri*)	9 g

Process　Soak the kelp and citron fruit in vinegar for 7 days.

Directions　Eat the 6 – 9 g kelp daily for 2 weeks successively.

Indications　Simple goiter.

Recipe 4
Ingredients

seaweed (*Sargassum*)	15 g
red sage root (*Radix Salviae Miltiorrhizae*)	15 g
curcuma root (*Radix Curcumae*)	9 g

  brown sugar   right amount

Process Decoct the first three ingredients in right amount of water, sift out the decoction from dregs, then season it with brown sugar.

Directions Take it one dose daily for 2 to 4 weeks successively.

Indications Simple goiter.

Recipe 5

Ingredients

 seaweed（Sargassum）   20 g
 kelp（Thallus Laminariae）   20 g
 laver   20 g
 Japanese sea tangle（Thallus Eckloniae） 20 g
 Chinese alpine rush   20 g

Process Decoct all them in right amount of water.

Directions Take it as drink.

Indications Simple goiter.

SECTION 19 Urinary Infection

Recipe 1
Ingredients
    talc (*Talcum*)　　　　　　　　30 – 60 g
    polished round – grained rice (*Semen Oryzae Sativae*)　　　　　　　　　　　　30 – 60 g

Process　Decoct the talc in water, sift out the decoction, add in the rice and go on cooking to make a gruel.

Directions　Take it before meal, once or twice daily.

Indications　Urinary infection.

Recipe 2
Ingredients
    lotus seed (*Semen Nelumbinis*)　　　50 g
    fresh liquorice (*Radix Glycyrrhizae*)　10 g

Process　Decoct all the ingredients in 500 ml of water over a slow fire until the lotus seed is soft, add in crystal sugar.

Directions　Eat the lotus seed and drink the soup.

Indications　Urinary infection.

Recipe 3

Ingredients

   knotgrass (*Herba Polygoni Avicularis*)
                                                15 – 20 g
   rehmannia root (*Radix Rehmanniae*)   15 g
   manshurian aristolochia stem (*Caulis Aristolochae Manshuriensis*)   10 g
   phellodendron bark (*Cortex Phellodendri*)   10 g
   liquorice (*Radix Glycyrrhizae*)   10 g
   isatis root (*Radix Isatidis*)   30 g
   rhubarb (*Radix et Rhizoma Rhei*)   6 g

Process   Decoct all them in water.

Directions   Take it in twice and one dose daily.

Indications   Urine system infections.

Chapter One

SECTION 20　Stone of Urinary System

Recipe 1

Ingredients

  walnut kernel (*Semen Juglandis*)　　500 g
 ·　*Chicken's gizzard - membrane* (*Endothelium Corneum Gigeriae Galli*)　　250 g
  honey (*Mel*)　　500 g

 Process　Decoct honey over fire until it becomes liquid completely. Add in walnut kernel and mix them well. Keep on decocting the mixture for 5 minutes. Store the mixture in a bottle for later use.

 Directions　Take one spoonful each time, three times daily.

 Indications　Stones of urinary system.

Recipe 2

Ingredients

  Lysimachia (*Herba Lysimachiae*)　　30 g
  red sage root (*Radix Salviae Miltiorrhizae*)
　　　　　　　　　　　　　　　　　　　30 g

talc (*Talcum*)	30 g
forsythia fruit (*Fructus Forsythiae*)	20 g
climbing fern spore	15 g
red peony root (*Radix Paeoniae Rubra*)	15 g
white cogongrass rhizome (*Rhizoma Imperatae*)	15 g
achyranthes root (*Radix Achyranthis Bidentatae*)	15 g
umbellate pore-fungus (*Polyporus Umbellatus*)	10 g

Process　Decoct the above ingredients in a right amount of water.

Directions　Take one dose of the decoction daily, one half in the morning and one half in the evening respectively.

Indications　Stones of urinary system.

Recipe 3

Ingredients

lygodium (*Spora Lygodii*)	15 g
green tea (*Folium Cameliae Viride*)	2 g

Process　Infuse them with boiling water in a cup.

Directions　Take a cup of it before breakfast at every morning and then take it as drink for 2 months successively.

Indications　Stone of urinary system.

Chapter One

Recipe 4

Ingredients

rhubarb (*Radix et Rhizoma Rhei*)	30 g
lygodium (*Spora Lygodii*)	30 g
egg several	

Process   Grind the first two ingredients into fine powder then make them into pills as large as mung bean with egg white.

Directions   Take it twice daily for 2 weeks successively, 5 g for each time.

Indications   Stone of urinary system.

Recipe 5

Ingredients

walnut kernel (*Semen Juglandis*)	120 g
crystal sugar	120 g
sesame oil	120 g

Process   Fry the walnut kernel in sesame oil until it become crimp, then ladle it out, grind it and sugar into fine powder, make it into paste with sesame oil.

Directions   Take it in twice for adult, in three times for child and one dose for three days.

Indications   Stone of urinary system.

SECTION 21 Nephritis

Recipe 1
Ingredients
  soft − shelled turtle   1
  Process Kill the soft − shelled turtle by soaking it in boiling water, then get rid of its head and jaw, then decoct it in water.
  Directions Take in once daily, one dose can be taken in three times.
  Indications Acute nephritis.

Recipe 2
Ingredients
  watermelon peel (*Exocarpium Citrulli*) 60 g
  white cogongrass rhizome (*Rhizoma Imperatae*)
                                             90 g
  Process Decoct them in right amount of water, sift out the decoction.
  Directions Take it in three times.
  Indications Nephritis with edema.

Recipe 3
Ingredients

    oldenlandis (*Herba Hedyotis Diffusae*)   20 g
    astragalus root (*Radix astragali seu Hedysari*)
        20 g
    white cogongrass rhizome (*Rhizoma Imperatae*)
        20 g
    motherwort (*Herba Leonuri*)   30 g
    red sage root (*Radix Salviae Miltiorrhizae*)
        15 g
    forsythia fruit (*Fructus Forsythiae*)   15 g
    tetrandra root (*Radix Stephaniae Tetrandrae*)
        6 g
    queen of the meadow (*Eupatorium*)   6 g

Process   Decoct all the ingredients in water.

Directions   Take the decoction in twice and one dose daily.

Indications   Acute nephritis.

Recipe 4
Ingredients

    corn stigma (*Stigma Maydis*)   30 g
    poria (*Poria*)   30 g
    white atractylodes rhizome (*Rhizoma Atractylodis Macrocephalae*)   15 g

Internal Diseases

    cinnamon twig (*Ramulus Cinnamomi*)   15 g
    purple perilla leaves (*Folium Perillae*)   15 g
    Chinese flowering quince (*Cydonia Lagenaria*)
                                                          15 g
    peel of areca seed (*Pericarpium Arecae*)   15 g
    plantain seed (*Semen Plantaginis*)   15 g

Process   Decoct all the ingredients in boiling water for 15 minutes, sift out the decoction from dregs; add in the water and decoct it again, then remove the dregs, mix the decoctions well.

Directions   Take the decoction in twice, one or two doses daily.

Indications   Acute nephritis.

Recipe 5
Ingredients
    crude astragalus root   30 g
    coix seed (*Semen Coicis*)   30 g
    polished glutinous rice (*Semen Oryzae Glutinosae*)
                                                       30 g
    red phaseolus bean (*Semen Phaseoli*)   15 g
    Chicken's gizzard – membrane (*Endothelium Corneum Gigeriae Galli*)   9 g
    dried tangerine (*Fructus Hordei*)   2

Process   Decoct the above ingredients in a right amount of water until it is done.

Directions   Take one dose daily.
Indications   Acute nephritis.

Recipe 6
Ingredients
    corn stigma (*Stigma Maydis*)   10 g
    corn (*Semen Maydis*)   20 stains
    cicada ecdysis   3
    snake slough (*Pillis Ophidiae*)   1
Process   Decoct all the ingredients in water.

Directions   Take the decoction. a month of administration consisted of one course.

Indications   Acute and chronic nephritis.

Recipe 7
Ingredients
    processed fish   500 g
    garlic (*Bulbus Allii*)   100 g
    white sugar   right amount
    whitealcoholic drinks   right amount
Process   Decoct all the ingredients in water.
Directions   Eat the meat and drink the soup.
Indications   Chronic nephritis.

SECTION 22　Impotency

Impotency is mostly due to sexual neurasthenia, with clinical manifestations of no or poor erection of penis and interference of normal sexual life.

Recipe 1
Ingredients
  pigeon egg   2
  longan pulp（*Arillus Longan*） 15 g
  wolfberry fruit（*Fructus Lycii*） 15 g
  schisandra fruit（*Fructus Schisandrae*） 15 g
  white sugar   right amount

Process　Get rid of the shell of the pigeon eggs, put it and other ingredients in a bowl, then steam it over water in a steamer.

Directions　Add in the sugar and take it as drink.

Indications　Impotency, lassitude, palpitation and emission.

Recipe 2

Chapter One

Ingredients

 deer testes   1 pair
 polished round − grained rice (*Semen Oryzae Sativae*)   100 g
 ginger, scallion, salt   right amount for each

Process Cut the testes of deer open, and get rid of its membrane, the cut it into threads, make them into gruel with rice, season it with gallic, ginger and salt.

Directions Take it before meal.

Indications Impotency.

Recipe 3

Ingredients

 cordyceps (*Cordyceps*)   10 g
 soft − shelled turtle (*Trioyx Sinensis*)   1000 g
 jujube (*Fructus Ziziphi Jujubae*)   20 g
 cooking wine   30 g
 salt, gourmet, scallion, ginger, garlic
          right amount for each
 soup of chicken   1000 g

Process Cut the soft − shell turtle into 4 sections, decoct them in water in a pot, when it come to boil, ladle them out, then cut the leg open and get rid of its oil, and clean them up. Soak the Chinese − date in boiling water. Put the soft − shell turtle in a big bowl and add in other ingredients in it, steam it over water in a steamer for 2 hours. Take the

Internal Diseases

big bowl out and remove the scallion and ginger.

    Directions   Take it with other foods.

    Indications   Impotency, emission, lassitude.

Chapter One

SECTION 23　Chronic Prostatitis

Chronic prostatitis is a very common disease of the urinary system in the young and middle-aged male patients, far more common than the acute one. With complicated clinical symptoms, it is hard to cure. The disease is usually a secondary infection of acute prostatitis or posterior urethritis. Sometimes, it may also be a secondary infection of the upper respiratory tract of mouth cavity. The common pathogens are staphylococcus, streptococcus; colibacillus, etc. It is often induced by excessive alcoholic drinking, injury of the perineum, excessive sexual intercourse. According to the usually seen white secretion from the urethra. This disease falls into the categories of "Jing zhuo" (turbid sperm) and " Lao lin" (stranguria induced by overstrain) in TCM.

ETIOLOGY AND PATHOGENESIS

The door of essence room is unlocked because of excessive sexual intercourse. Damp-heat takes the opportunity to occupy the room, forcing sperm to flow to the urinary bladder and leave the body along with urine. Then, there will result deficiency of the kidney-Yin, hyperactivity of the ministerial fire, disturbance of essence room and retention of fire all of which get together to lead to stagnation of Qi and blood in the spermatic duct and cause this disease at last. If the disease course is prolonged, the deficient Yin will involve Yang. At this time, there will occur syndrome due to insufficiency of the kidney-Yang.

Main Symptoms and Signs

White and turbid trip from the urethral meatus commonly seen at the end of urination to in the course of having a bowel movement with one's strength, or white sticky secretion from the urethral meatus usually found after getting up in the morning; frequent urination and burning urine and stabbing and itching urethra existing in most cases; tenesmus and distension and pain in the lower abdomen, lumbosacral portion, perineum and testes; listlessness, acratia, dizziness, insomnia, sexual hypoesthesia, spermatorrhea, prospermia, impotence and hemospermia.

MAIN POINTS OF DIAGNOSIS

1. Symptoms

1) Urinary Symptoms: There is frequent and urgent micturition, pain in micturition and a uncomfortable urination or a burning feeling in micturition. At the end of urination or in moving the bowels, there is some sticky liquid dripping from the urethra.

2) Pain: There is a dull or a distending pain in the perineum and inside the rectum. The pain may radiate to the

lumbosacral portion, the hip, the thigh, the testicle, the groin, etc.

3) Disturbance of Sexual Function: It is marked by sexual hypoesthesia, impotence, prospermia, pain in ejaculation, hemospermia, nocturnal emission, etc.

4) Constitutional Symptoms: There are neurasthenic symptoms such as weakness and fatigue in the whole body, aching pain at the waist and the back, insomnia, dreaminess, etc. Sometimes, diseases such as arthritis, endocarditis, iritis, conjunctivitis and peripheral neuritis may be initiated.

2. Examination

1) Rectal Examination: This examination elicits a swollen prostate with tumefaction and obvious tenderness. Sometimes, the prostate may be hard and smaller than the usual size. The surface may be uneven and feels as if here are nodes on it. But it can also be normal at times.

2) Examination of Prostatic Fluid: Massage the prostate to collect prostatic fluid and examine it through microscopy. In a serious case there will be a lot of pus cells and more than 10 white cells present in each high power field. On the other hand, the lecithin corpuscles will obviously decrease or disappear.

3) The Three–glass Urine Test: If there are pus cells in the first glass and none in the second and the third glass or there are pus cells in the first and the third glass and none in

the second that means the infection probably comes from the prostate.

4) Bacterial Culture; After douching to sterilize and clean the urethra, massage prostate to collect the prostatic fluid for bacterial culture.

5) Use smear examination to find bacteria.

Recipe 1
Ingredients
    earthworm (*Lumbricus*)   20 g
    giant knot (*weed Rhizome*)   20 g
    pangolin scales (*Squama Manitis*)   20 g
    radish seed (*Semen Raphani*)   20 g
    astragalus root (*Radix astragali seu Hedysari*)
        30 g
    liquorice (*Radix Glycyrrhizae*)   10 g
    manshurian aristolochia stem (*Caulis Aristolochae Manshuriensis*)   15 g
    plantain seed (*Semen Plantaginis*)   15 g

Process   Decoct all them in water.
Directions   Take the decoction in twice, one dose daily.
Indications   Chronic prostatitis.

Recipe 2
Ingredients

white orchid	30 g
lean pork	200 g
salt	right amount

Process   Clean the pork lean and cut it into cubes, decoct it in right amount of water in a pot, when it come to boil, add in the and go on cooking until the meat it will done, season it with salt.

Directions   Eat the meat and drink the soup.

Indications   Chronic prostatitis.

SECTION 24 Hyperplasia of Prostate

Hyperplasia of prostate, also known as prostatic hyperplasia, is a very common disease that occurs in old male patients. Generally, this disease is considered to be associate with the disturbance of sexual hormones. The main manifestations are uroschesis and difficulty of urination. It belongs to the category of "long Bi" (retention of urine) in TCM.

ETIOLOGY AND PATHOGENESIS

The urinary bladder works as if it were a state officer in change of the storage of water. When it is in good condition, urination will be normal. Dysfunction of it leads to uroschesis. So the pathologic change of hyperplasia of prostate takes place in the urinary bladder. However, normal smooth urination is dependent on the normal function of tri-Jiao and the normal function of tri-Jiao relies on the lung, spleen and kidney. For instance, dysfunction of the lung (the upper-Jiao) in descending makes water passages fail to be drained, which prevents water from flowing to the bladder. Disorder of the spleen and stomach (the middle-Jiao) leads to accumulation of damp-heat in the bladder. In addition, deficiency of the Qi of the kidney (the lower-Jiao) results in imbalance between Yin and Yang, which also influences the bladder. In short, disturbance of any of the above organs will, in the end, cause anuresis, uneven urination, enuresis and urinary incontinence. Moreover, symptoms such as anuresis may be induced due to accumulation of blood in the bladder. for the blood stasis will block water passages.

Main Symptoms and Signs:

Slow onset, frequent urination occurring in the early stage which is especially obvious in the night, difficulty in urination appearing after the symptom frequent urination, urination taking place after long waiting, dribbing of urine at the end of urination which gives the feeling that the urination is not complete. Urinating in fraction because of incomplete urination, urination becoming more difficult as the obstructure is getting ever so severe, urinating within short range, thin urine scream, more and more urine retained in the bladder which is often distended so as to cause chronic uroschesis, even voluntary micturation (false urinary incontinence) or enuresis in the night, great amount of hematuria occasionally seen when the superficial cirsoid phleborrhexis of the neck of the bladder and symptoms due to acute uroschesis or irritation to the bladder all of which are induced by overstrain, affection of cold, excess of sexual intercourse, over-intake of pungent or irritant food or secondary infection of the bladder raised blood pressure, acratia, dizziness, vertigo, poor appetite, and complications of pile, hernia, proctoptosis and hematochezia.

MAIN POINTS OF DIAGNOSIS

1. It occurs mostly in aged people who are over 50.

2. Symptoms

1) Frequent Micturition: This is a symptom at the early stage of the disease. Gradually, the frequency of urination increases, which is obvious especially at night. In mild cases the urination will happen 4 - 5 times a night and in serious cases it may occur dozens of times.

2) Difficulty in Urination: At the beginning, the patient has to wait for a while before urination. Later on, the obstructional condition becomes more serious, accompanied with difficulty in urination, weak and thready stream of urine, then interruption or even dribbling in urination.

3) Acute Uroschesis: This symptom is due to factors such as constipation, cold, alcoholic drinking and weariness which can cause hyperemia and hydrops of the neck of the urinary bladder. Complete obstruction may be formed and acute uroschesis will result.

4) Urinary Incontinence: When the filling of the urinary bladder reaches an extreme state and the sphincter muscule of urethra, urine will dribble out continuously from the urethra. This phenomenon is called pseudo - uroschesis.

5) Hematuria: Because of the hyperemia of the neck of urinary bladder, sometimes, hematuria may be found under

microscopy or even by gross inspection.

6) Complications: On the one hand, urinary obstruction for a long time may lead to other sicknesses like decrease of renal functions or even renal failure, manifested as loss of appetite, fatigue, then nausea and vomiting, hypertension and anemia. Finally, a coma will follow. On the other hand, a long term difficulty in urination may also cause the increase of the abdominal pressure and produce inguinal hernia, hemorrhoid, proctoptosis, varicose vein in he lower limbs and so on.

3. Examination

1) Digital Examination of Rectum: Prior to the examination, the contents in the urinary bladder should be entirely cleared out. The examination often shows that the prostate gland is larger than usual but its surface is smooth with no nodes on it. Its edge is distinct and the hardness is medium with resilience. The central sulcus becomes shallow or disappears.

2) Residual Urinary Test: The residual urine is the amount of remaining urine which is collected by urethal catheterization immediately after urination.

3) Cystoscopy and Cystography: If the middle lobe of the prostate increases in size, it is necessary to go through cystoscopy and cystography in order to confirm the diagnosis.

4) Ultrasonic Examination: This examination will show

the volume, form and internal structure of the prostate gland.

5) Laboratory Examination: Throngh routine uroscopy, pus cells or red blood cells may be found. Prolonged urinary retention may influence the function of the kidney. Therefore, a further test of urea nitrogen and creatinine will be required.

Recipe 1
Ingredients
white   10 g
black edible fungus (*Auricularia*)   10 g
crystal sugar   30 g

Process   Soak the first ingredients in warm water, clean them up, put them in a bowl, add in crystal and right amount of water, steam them over water in a steamer.

Directions   Take it twice, one dose daily for a week successively.

Indications   Hyperplasia of prostate, or prostatomegaly.

Recipe 2
Ingredients
dangshen (*Radix Codonopsis Pilosulae*)
    250 g

astragalus root (*Radix astragali seu Hedysari*)	
	250 g
white sugar	500 g

Process　Decoct the first ingredients in water for 30 minutes, sift out the decoction from dregs; add water in the dregs, repeat this process for 3 times, mix the decoctions, enrich it until it become sticky, let it cool, add in the sugar and mix it well, dry it under the sun, put it in a china bottle for latter use.

Directions　Infuse it with boiling water. Take it twice daily, 10 g for each time.

Indications　Hyperplasia of prostate, or prostatomegaly.

Recipe 3

Ingredients

dangshen (*Radix Codonopsis Pilosulae*)	10 g
Chinese - date (*Fructus Ziziphi Jujubae*)	
	20 g
polished glutinous rice (*Semen Oryzae Glutinosae*)	250 g
white sugar	50 g

Process　Decoct the first ingredients in water for 30 minutes, sift out the decoction from dregs, then add in the sugar and go on cooking until it become sticky extract. Stew the rice in water, when it is well done, add in the sticky extract.

Internal Diseases

Directions   Take it as main food in meals.
Indications   Hyperplasia of prostate, or prostatomegaly.

Chapter One

SECTION 25 Headache

Headache is a kind of clinically common – subjective symptom. It can be accompanied by various kinds of acute and chronic diseases. This section will mainly discuss some symptoms characterized mainly by headache.

I. CLINICAL MANIFESTATIONS

1. Headache due to Exopathy
1) Headache due to Pathogenic Wind – Cold Pathogen: frequent headache, pain extending to the nape and back, aversion to cold and wind, joy for head – binding, no thirst, thin and whitish tongue fur, floating and tense pulse.

2) Headache due to Pathogenic Wind – Heat: distension and pain in the head, fever, aversion to wind, thirst with desire to drink, dark urine, reddened tongue with thin and yellow fur, floating and rapid pulse.

3) Headache due to Pathogenic Summer – Heat and Dampness: strong binding pain in the head, lassitude of limbs, poor appetite, fullness in the epigastric region, fever,

sweating, dysphoria, thirst, greasy fur and slippery pulse.

2. HEADACHE DUE TO INTERNAL INJURY

1) Headache due to Abnormal Ascending of Liver – Yang: headache with intermittent dizziness, dysphoria, irritability, insomnia, bitter taste, reddened tongue with thin and yellow fur, taut and forceful pulse.

2) Headache due to Stagnation of Phlegm: Headache with dizziness, fullness in the epigastric region, vomiting, abundant expectoration, whitish and greasy fur, slippery or taut and slippery pulse.

3) Headache due to Deficiency of Blood: Headache and dizziness which become intense with slight labor, weakness, dysphoria, palpitation, shortness of breath, pale complexion, pale tongue with thin and whitish fur, thready and feeble pulse.

4) Headache due to Deficiency of Kidney: Headache with a sensation of emptiness inside the head, dizziness, weakness and lassitude in the loin and legs, emission, leukorrhagia, tinnitus, insomnia, reddened tongue with little fur, thready and feeble pulse.

II. DIFFERENTIATION

1. Headache due to invasion of pathogenic wind into the

channels and collaterals: Headache occurs often, especially on exposure to wind. The pain may extend to the nape of the neck and back regions. Thin and white tongue coating, floating pulse.

2. Headache due to upsurge of liver — yang: headache, distension of the head, irritability, hot temper, dizziness, blurring of vision, red tongue with thin and yellow coating, taut and rapid pulse.

3. Headache due to deficiency of both qi and blood: Lingering headache, dizziness, blurring of vision, lassitude, lusterless face, pale tongue with thin and white coating, thin and weak pulse.

Recipe 1

Ingredients

pig's brain	1
gastrodia tuber (*Rhizoma Gastrodiae*)	2 g

Process　Grind the gastrodia tuber into fine powder, then decoct it and pig's brain in right amount of water over a slow fire for an hour, when it become sticky soup, remove the dregs.

Directions　Eat the pig's brain and drink the soup. Take it in twice, one dose for a day.

Indications　Headache.

Recipe 2

Ingredients

 longan pulp (*Arillus Longan*)   100 g
 egg   2
 white sugar   right amount

Process Pound the dried longan aril into pieces, then decoct them with eggs in right amount of water, remove the shell of eggs, go on heat it over a slow fire for an hour, add in the sugar.

Directions Eat eggs and drink the soup. Take it in twice and one dose daily.

Indications Headache.

Recipe 3

Ingredients

 cimicifuga rhizome (*Rhizoma Cimicifugae*)
              18 g
 rehmannia root (*Radix Rehmanniae*)   15 g
 tea (*Thea*)   12 g
 scutellaria root (*Radix Scutellariae*)   3 g
 coptis root (*Rhizoma Coptidis*)   3 g
 bupleurum root (*Radix Bupleuri*)   8 g
 dahurian Angelica root (*Radix Angelicae Dahuricae*)   6 g

Chapter One

Process　Decoct all them in right amount of water, sift out the decoction from dregs.

Directions　Take the decoction at once time, one dose daily.

Indications　Headache.

Internal Diseases

SECTION 26 Dizziness

Recipe 1
Ingredients

　fresh reed Rhizome（*Rhizoma Phragmitis*）
　　　　　　　　　　　　　　　　90 g
　bamboo shaving（*Caulis Bambusae in Taeniam*）
　　　　　　　　　　　　　　　　4.5 g
　parched hawthorn　　　　　　9 g
　parched rice sprout（*Fructus Oryzae Germinatus*）
　　　　　　　　　　　　　　　　9 g
　red tangerine peel（*Exocarpium Citri Reticulatae*）
　　　　　　　　　　　　　　　　2.4 g
　frosted mulberry leaf（*Folium Mori*）　6 g

　Process　Cut the fresh reed rhizome into pieces, them grind it with other ingredients into raw powder, decoct them in right amount of water.

　Directions　Take it as drink, one dose daily.
　Indications　Dizziness.

Recipe 2

Chapter One

Ingredients

    chrysanthemum (*Flos Chrysanthemi*)   9 g
    mulberry leaf (*Folium Mori*)   9 g
    ophiopogon root (*Radix Ophiopogonis*)   9 g
    antelope's horn (*Cornu Saigae Tataricae*)
                                                     1.5 g
    poria (*Poria*)   12 g
    parched fruit of citron (*Fructus Aurantii*)
                                                     4.5 g
    fresh reed Rhizome (*Rhizoma Phragmitis*) 2

Process Cut the fresh reed rhizome into pieces, them grind it with other ingredients into raw powder, decoct them in right amount of water.

Directions Take it warmly as drink, once daily.

Indications Dizziness.

Recipe 3

Ingredients

    chicken   250 g
    fleece-flower root (*Radix Polygoni Multiflori*)
                                                     15 - 20 g
    Chinese angelica root (*Radix Angelicae Sinensis*)
                                                     12 - 15 g
    wolfberry fruit (*Fructus Lycii*)   15 g
    salt   right amount

Process Cut the chicken meat into cubes, decoct them

with other ingredients in right amount of water over a strong fire, when it come to boil, go on heat it over a slow fire until the meat is well done, season it with salt.

Directions Eat the meat and drink the soup. Take it with other foods.

Indications dizziness and lassitude.

Recipe 4
Ingredients
 black soybean   50 g
 Chinese - date (*Fructus Ziziphi Jujubae*)
                50 g
 longan pulp (*Arillus Longan*)   15 g

Process Decoct them in 3 bowls of water until 2 bowls of decoction left.

Directions Take it in twice, one dose daily.

Indications Dizziness.

Recipe 5
Ingredients
 ginkgo nut (*Semen Ginkgo*)   6 g
 longan pulp (*Arillus Longan*)   7

Process Decoct them in right amount of water.

Directions Take the decoction before breakfast, one dose daily.

Indications Dizziness.

Chapter One

SECTION 27　Insomnia

Recipe 1

Ingredients

    dried longan pulp（*Arillus Longan*）　15 g

    euryal seed（*Semen Euryales*）　15 g

    polished round – grained rice（*Semen Oryzae Sativae*）　100 g

    lotus seed without pith（*Semen Nelumbinis*）　6 g

    white sugar　right amount

Process　Stew the euryal seed in water, when it is done, remove its shell, pound it into stains, make it and rice, lotus seed without pith litchi arial and right amount of water into gruel. Season it with sugar.

Directions　Take it one dose daily.

Indications　Insomnia and neurosis.

Recipe 2

Ingredients

    dangshen（*Radix Codonopsis Pilosulae*）　60 g

Internal Diseases

    scrophularia root (*Radix Scrophulariae*) 30 g
    amber (*Succinum*)   18 g
    cinnabar (*Cinnabaris*)   12 g
    ophiopogon root (*Radix Ophiopogonis*) 12 g

Process   Grind all the ingredients into fine powder. Infuse the fine powder with boiling water.

Directions   Take it at bedtime, 3 to 5 grams of fine powder each time.

Indications   Insomnia.

Recipe 3

Ingredients

    euryal seed (*Semen Euryales*)   6 g
    coix seed (*Semen Coicis*)   6 g
    white hyacinth bean (*Semen Dolichoris*) 6 g
    lotus seed (*Semen Nelumbinis*)   6 g
    Chinese yam (*Rhizoma Dioscoreae*)   6 g
    jujube (*Fructus Ziziphi Jujubae*)   6 g
    longan (*Arillus Longan*)   6 g
    lily bulb (*Bulbus Lilii*)   6 g
    round - polished glutinous rice (*Semen Oryzae Sativae*)   150 g
    sugar   right amount

Process   Decoct the first eight ingredients in right amount of water for 40 minutes, add in the rice and go on cooking until it is well done. Season it with sugar.

Directions Take it in several times, take it one dose daily for several days successively.

Indications Insomnia.

Recipe 4

Ingredients

lotus seed（*Semen Nelumbinis*）	30 g
longan（*Arillus Longan*）	30 g
jujube（*Fructus Ziziphi Jujubae*）	20 g
crystal sugar	right amount

Process Soak the lotus seed in water, remove its pith and peel, then decoct them with litchi arial and Chinese-date in right amount of water in an earthenware pot over a slow fire, when it is well done, add in crystal sugar.

Directions Take it once or twice weekly.

Indications Insomnia and neurosis, palpitation, forgetfulness, anemia.

SECTION 28 Diabetes

Clinical diabetes mellitus represents a syndrome with disordered metabolism and inappropriate hyperglycemia due to either an absolute deficiency of insulin secretion or a reduction in its biologic effectiveness or both and leading to metabolic disturbance of carbohydrate, fat and protein. The disease os frequently followed by water − electrolyte imbalance and acid − base disturbance. According to the age of the patients, clinical manifestation and requirements for insulin, diabetes mellitus can be divided into many types.

The national institutes of health in 1979 decided to defer a "functional" classification of diabetes that based upon insulin secretion characteristics of insulin sensitivity. It recommends classifying diabetes mellitus into 2 major types. A. Type I. Insulin − Dependent Diabetes Mellitus (IDDM). This severe form is associated with ketosis in the untreated state. It occurs most commonly in juveniles but also occasionally in adults.

B. Type II. Non − Insulin − Dependent Diabetes Mellitus (NIDDM). This represents a heterogeneous group comprising milder forms of diabetes that occur predominantly in adults but occasionally in juveniles. Two subgroups of patients with Type II diabetes are currently distinguished by the absence or presence of obesity.

a. Nonobese NIDDM patients. These patients generally show an absent or blunted early phase of insulin release in response to glucose.

b. Obese NIDDM patients. This form of diabetes is secondary to extrapancreatic factors that produce insensitivity to endogenous insulin.

In traditional Chinese medicine, the modern term for the condition is "emaciation - thirst disease", but in ancient Chinese medicine, it is called "Shi Yi" or "Xiao Dan". The diagnosis is mainly based on symptoms such as thirst, polydipsia, polyphagia, emaciation and polyuria.

ETIOLOGY AND PATHOGENESIS

Diabetes occurs in association with the following etiologic factors:

1. The spleen and stomach are damaged by overeating greasy food or by overconsuming alcohol causing failure of the spleen in transporting and transforming which, in turn, causes interior - heat to accumulate and consume food and body fluids, finally resulting in diabetes.

2. Impairment of body fluid

Deficiency of Yin and over - intake of rich fatty food and liquor contribute to accumulation of heat in the interior.

The accumulated heat tends to turn to dryness. The dryness will impair body fluid.

3. Anxiety, anger and mental depression injure the liver, causing liver qi to stagnate. Protractedly stagnated liver qi turn into pathogenic heat which costumes body fluids and eventually leads to deabetes.

4. Deficiency in the kidneys caused by intemperance in sexual life or congenital essence defect causes kidney qi to wane; as a result, kidney qi fails to maintain the function of the bladder in restraining urine discharge, thus polyuria occurs.

5. Burned Yin – fluid of the lung and stomach

long – term of emotional stimulus leads to stagnation of Qi. Stagnation of Qi leads to production of fire . The fire burns Yin – fluid of the lung and stomach.

6. Attack of the lung and stomach by hyperactive fire

Overstrain and sexual intemperance exhaust Yin – essence. Exhaustion of Yin – essence causes deficiency of Yin. Yin – deficiency results in hyperactivity of fire. The resulting fire will go upward to heat the lung and stomach.

Main Symptoms and Signs

The classic symptoms of polyuria, thirst, recurrent blurred vision, parenthesis and fatigue are manifestations of hyperglycemia and thus are common to both major types of diabetes , likewise, pruritus vulvae and vaginitis are frequent initial complaints of adult females with hyperglycemia and glycosuria due to either absolute or relative deficiencies of insulin. Weight loss despite normal or increased appetite is a feature of IDDM, whereas weight loss os unusual in obese patients with NIDDM who have normal or increased levels of circulating insulin. These latter patients with the insulin − insensitive type of diabetes may be relatively asymptomatic and may be detected only after glycosuria or hyperglycemia is noted during a routine examination. Diabetes should be suspected in obese patients, in those with a positive family history of deabetes, in patients presenting with peripheral neuropathy and in women who have delivered large babies or had polyhydramnios, preeclampsia, or unexplained fetal losses.

MAIN POINTS OF DIAGNOSIS

1. The characteristics of a typical case of diabetes mellitus are often polyphagia, polydipsia, polyuria and loss of body weight. Early or asymptomatic patients only show abnormal release of cortical hormone and insulin inside the body. The level of fasting blood sugar is elevated with abnormal glucose tolerance test. Symptomatic patients are frequently complicated by other symptoms of dermal, neural and endocrinous disorders, besides polyphogia, polydipsia, polyuria and loss of body weight.

2. The main complications and concomitant diseases of diabetes mellitus are diabetic ketoacidosis , cardiovascular diseases, diabetic renopathy and peripheral neuropathy. Cardiovascular complications art the chief causes of death.

3. Diabetes mellitus is classified into juvenile and adult types according to the clinical features. The age of onset of the juvenile type is young and has a tendency to inheritance. Blood sugar fluctuates widely and is quote sensitive to insulin. Treatment is difficult and is easily complicated by ketoacidosis and hypoglycemia, and so it is often named insulin − depending diabetes or unstable diabetes. The age of onset of adult type is above 40. This type is relatively mild and can be controlled by dietary restriction or oral antidiabetics. Therefore it is also named non − insulin depending diabetes or stable diabetes.

4. Accessory examination

(1) Fasting blood − glucose is higher than 130 − 140 mg/dl. Blood glucose after meal is more than 160 − 180 mg/dl. Urine is positive for glucose. If complicated by ketoses, urine is positive for ketone bodies.

(2) Fasting plasma glucose is less than 140 mg/dl in suspected cases. A standardized oral glucose tolerance test may be done. Glucose tolerance test can be used to diagnose early or suspected cases and is the principal test in diagnosis.

The national Diabetes Data Group recommends giving a 75g glucose dose dissolved in 300ml of water for adults (1.75 per kg ideal body weight for children) after an over − night fast in subjects who have been receiving at least 150 − 200g of carbohydrate daily for 3 days before the test.

Normal glucose tolerance is considered to be present

when the 2 - hour plasma glucose is less than 140 mg/dl, with no value between zero time and 2 hours exceeding 200 mg/dl. However, a diagnosis of diabetes mellitus requires plasma glucose levels to be 200 mg/dl both at 2 hours and at least twice between zero time and 2 hours.

(3) New diagnostic techniques such as testing blood insulin levels are quit helpful in understanding the pathological changed of pancreas and in obtaining information concerning treatment.

Insulin levels during glucose tolerance test. Normal immunoreactive insulin levels range from less than 10 to 25 uv/ml in the fasting state and 50 to 130 uv/ml at 1 hour and usually return to levels below 100uv/ml by 2 hours. A value below 50uv/ml at 1 hour and less than 100uv/ml at 2 hours in the presence of sustained hyperglycemia implicates insensitivity of B cells to glucose as the cause of hyperglycemia, whereas levels substantially above 100uv/ml at these times suggest tissue unresponsiveness to the action of insulin.

Recipe 1

Ingredients

    glehnia root (*Radix Glehniae*)   15 g
    ophiopogon root (*Radix Ophiopogonis*) 15 g
    rehmannia root (*Radix Rehmanniae*)   15 g
    fragrant solomonseal rhizome (*Rhizoma Polygo-*

Internal Diseases

nati Odorati)   5 g

Process   Grind all them into raw powder, then decoct them in water and sift out the decoction from dregs.

Directions   Take it as drink, one dose daily.

Indications   Diabetes.

Recipe 2

Ingredients

    spinach root   100 g

    tremella (*tremella*)   10 g

Process   Decoct them in right amount of water.

Directions   Take it as drink twice daily.

Indications   Diabetes with thirst.

Recipe 3

Ingredients

    spinach root   250 g

    Chicken's gizzard - membrane (*Endothelium Corneum Gigeriae Galli*)   10 g

    round - polished glutinous rice (*Semen Oryzae Sativae*)   50 g

Process   Cut the root of the spinach into pieces and decoct them with membrane of chicken's gizzard in water, when it is well done, add in the rice and go on cooking to make a gruel.

Directions   Take it in. twice daily.

Indications Diabetes.

Recipe 4
Ingredients

> *fragrant solomonseal rhizome* (*Rhizoma Polygonati Odorati*)　　　　　　　　　　15 – 20 g
> *polished round-grained rice* (*Semen Oryzae Sativae*)　　　　　　　　　　100 g
> *crystal sugar*　　　　　　　right amount

Process Clean up the fragrant solomonseal rhizome, remove its stigma and root, cut it into pieces and decoct it in right amount of water, sift out the decoction from dregs, then add in rice and right amount of water, go on cooking it over a slow fire to make a gruel, when it is well done, add in the crystal sugar and go on cooking for one or two boils.

Directions Take it twice daily, one administration course consists of 5 – 7 days.

Indications Diabetes.

Recipe 5
Ingredients

> *wolfberry bark* (*Cortex Lycii Radicis*)　30 g
> *mulberry bark* (*Cortex Mori Radicis*)　15 g
> *ophiopogon root* (*Radix Ophiopogonis*)　15 g
> *flour*　　　　　　　　　　　　　　100 g

Process Decoct the first ingredients in right amount of water, sift out the decoction from dregs, then add in the flour of wheat to make a thin gruels.

Directions   Take it once daily.

Indications   Diabetes.

Recipe 6

Ingredients

    parched atractylodes rhizome (*Rhizoma Atractylodis*)   20 - 40 g

    parched white atractylodes rhizome (*Rhizoma Atractylodis Macrocephalae*)   15 - 30 g

    Chinese yam (*Rhizoma Dioscoreae*)   30 - 50 g

    crude astragalus root   30 - 50 g

    glehnia root (*Radix Glehniae*)   30 - 40 g

    scrophularia root (*Radix Scrophulariae*)   15 - 30 g

    mantis egg - case (*Ootheca Mantidis*)   10 - 15 g

    schisandra fruit (*Fructus Schisandrae*)   15 - 25 g

    fragrant solomonseal rhizome (*Rhizoma Polygonati Odorati*)   20 - 40 g

Process   Decoct all them in right amount of water for three times, sift out the decoction from dregs and mix them well.

Directions   Take it as drink, one dose daily.

Indications Diabetes.

Recipe 7
Ingredients

    astragalus root（*Radix astragali seu Hedysari*）
                                                        50 g
    dangshen（*Radix Codonopsis Pilosulae*）30 g
    rehmannia root（*Radix Rehmanniae*）25 g
    Chinese yam（*Rhizoma Dioscoreae*）25 g
    fragrant solomonseal rhizome（*Rhizoma Polygonati Odorati*）20 g
    wolfberry fruit（*Fructus Lycii*）20 g
    lucid asparagus root（*Radix Asparagi*）20 g
    scrophularia root（*Radix Scrophulariae*）20 g
    dodder seed（*Semen Cascade*）15 g
    glossy privet fruit（*Fructus Ligustri Lucidi*）
                                                       15 g

Process Soak them in right amount of water, decoct them in water for twice, sift out the decoctions and mix them well.

Directions Take the decoction as drink, one dose daily.

Indications Diabetes.

Recipe 8
Ingredients

root of American ginseng (Radix Panacis Quinquefolii)　　3 g
　　　ophiopogon root (Radix Ophiopogonis)　10 g
　　　lophatherum gracile (Folium Bambusae Lophatheri)　　6 g
　　　round - polished glutinous rice (Semen Oryzae Sativae)　　30 g

Process　Decoct the ophiopogon root and lophatherum in right amount of water, remove the dregs, add in the rice and go on cooking, when it is nearly done, add in the slices of the root of American ginseng.

Directions　Take the gruel.

Indications　Diabetes with thirst, dryness of mouth and short breath, lassitude and fatigue.

Chapter Two Surgical Diseases

SECTION 1 Furuncle, carbuncle, and cellulitis

Recipe 1
Ingredients

Radix astragali seu Hedysari	30 g
Radix Angelicae Sinensis	10 g
jujube (Fructus Ziziphi Jujubae)	10 g

Process Decoct them in right amount of water for 40 minutes, then sift out the decoction from dregs; add right amount of water into dregs, and go on cooking for 30 minutes, sift out the decoction, put the decoctions together.

Directions Take the decoction in twice daily, both in the morning and in the evening. One dose daily.

Indications Furuncle, carbuncle, and cellulitis.

Recipe 2
Ingredients

flower of cottonrose hibiscus	30 – 60 g
crystal sugar	15 g

Surgical Diseases

Process   Decoct the lotus flower in right amount of water, sift out the decoction from dregs, then dissolve the crystal sugar in it.

Directions   Take it as drink.

Indications   Furuncle, carbuncle, and cellulitis.

Recipe 3

Ingredients

honeysuckle flower (*Flos Lonicerae*)	30 g
liquorice (*Radix Glycyrrhizae*)	3 g
mung bean (*Semen Phaseoli Radiati*)	15 g

Process   Decoct them in right amount of water, then sift out the decoction from dregs.

Directions   Take it as drink.

Indications   Furuncle, carbuncle, and cellulitis.

Recipe 4

Ingredients

fresh luffa (*Fructus Luffae*)	1

Process   Cut luffa into pieces, then pound them into mash and extract the juice.

Directions   Spread it on the affected part frequently.

Indications   Furuncle, carbuncle, and cellulitis.

SECTION 2 Scrofula

Recipe 5
Ingredients

    prunella spike (*Spica Prunellae*)   30 g
    honeysuckle flower (*Flos Lonicerae*)   30 g
    viola herb (*Herba Violae*)   30 g
    crystal sugar   right amount

Process Grind all them into raw powder, then decoct them in water and sift out the decoction from dregs, dissolve the crystal sugar in it.

Directions Take it as drink, one dose daily.

Indications Tuberculosis of cervical lymph nodes.

Recipe 6
Ingredients

    laver   30 g
    white radish (*Napus*)   250 g
    dried orange peel (*Pericarpium Citri*)   3 g

Process Cut the white radish into slices, then tear the laver into pieces, decoct them with dried orange peel in right amount water.

Directions Take it in twice, one dose every other day for 2 weeks successively.

Indications Tuberculosis of cervical lymph nodes.

SECTION 3 Acute Mastitis

Recipe 1
Ingredients
 honeysuckle flower (*Flos Lonicerae*) 30 g
 viola herb (*Herba Violae*) 30 g

Process Decoct all them in water, when it is done, sift out the decoction from the dregs.

Directions Take it as drink, one dose daily.

Indications Acute mastitis.

Recipe 2
Ingredients
 chrysanthemum flower (*Flos Chrysanthemi*)
             5 g
 liquorice (*Radix Glycyrrhizae*) 25 g
 white sugar right amount

Process Infuse the first two ingredients with boiling water, then season it with sugar.

Directions Take it as drink, one dose daily.

Indications Acute mastitis.

Recipe 3

Ingredients

    jujube (*Fructus Ziziphi Jujubae*)   10

    fresh Chinese yam (*Rhizoma Dioscoreae*)   100 g

    polished round-grained rice (*Semen Oryzae Sativae*)   250 g

Process   Make them into gruel with right amount of water.

Directions   Take it twice daily for five days successively.

Indications   Acute mastitis.

Recipe 4

Ingredients

    peach kernel (*Semen Persicae*)   3

    bulb of edible tulip (*Orithyia Edulis*)   5 g

    millet wine   right amount

Process   Pound the walnut kernel into mash, grind the bulb of edible tulip into fine powder, then mix them well.

Directions   Take it with millet wine, two dose daily for 3 days.

Indications   Acute mastitis.

Recipe 5

Ingredients

 rhubarb (Radix et Rhizoma Rhei) 10 g
 ground beetle 10 g
 root of Chinese clematis (Radix Clematidis)
  10 g
 bulb of edible tulip (Orithyia Edulis) 10 g
 arisaema (Rhizoma Arisaematis) 10 g
 ginger (Zingiberis) pinellia tuber (Rhizoma Pinelliae) 10 g
 seed of garden balsam (Semen Biotae) 15 g
 knoxia root (Radix Knoxiae) 5 g
 aucklandia root (Radix Aucklandiae) 5 g
 glove (Flos Caryophylli) 5 g

Process Grind all them into fine powder, then mix them well and put it in a bottle for latter use.

Directions Make it into paste with millet wine or water, and apply it on the affected part with the gauze cloth.

Indications Acute mastitis.

SECTION 4 Hernia

Recipe 1
Ingredients
   aniseed (*Fructus Foeniculi*)   10 – 15 g
   polished round – grained rice (*Semen Oryzae Sativae*)   30 – 60 g

Process   Decoct the aniseed in right amount water, remove the dregs, add in the rice and go on cooking to make a gruel.

Directions   Take it before meals.
Indications   Hernia.

Recipe 2
Ingredients
   lychee – pit (*Semen Litchi*)   10 g
   olive – pit (*Nucleus Olivaris*)   10 g

Process   Pound them into pieces, then soak them in boiling water.

Directions   Take it as drink.
Indications   Hernia.

Recipe 3

Ingredients

    lychee − pit (*Semen Litchi*)   10 − 15 g
    tangerine seed (*Semen Citri Reticulatae*)
                                      10 − 15 g
  brown sugar   ·   right amount

Process   Decoct the first ingredients in water, remove the dregs. Season it with brown sugar.

Directions   Take it warmly as drink.

Indications   Hernia.

SECTION 5 Hemorrhoids

Recipe 1
Ingredients
    xanthium（*Fructus Xanthii*）   15 g
    polished round－grained rice（*Semen Oryzae Sativae*）   150 g

Process Parch xanthium over a slow fire until it becomes yellowish, add 200 ml water and go on cooking until 100 ml of the decoction left, then sift out the decoction from dregs. Add the rice and 400 ml of water in the decoction and go on cooking to make a thin gruel.

Directions Take it warmly, twice a day.
Indications Hemorrhoids.

Recipe 2
Ingredients
    Radix Sophorae Flavescentis   60 g
    brown sugar   60 g
    egg   2

Process Decoct the first ingredient in right amount of

water, remove the dregs, then add in the brown sugar and stew the eggs in it until it is done.

Directions　Take the eggs and drink the soup at once time. one dose daily for a week successively.

Indications　Hemorrhoids.

Recipe 3
Ingredients
　　Radix Sophorae Flavescentis　　　　60 g
　　prickly ash peel（Pericarpium Zanthozxyli）
　　　　　　　　　　　　　　　　　　60 g
　　alum　　　　　　　　　　　　　90 g

Process　Decoct all them in 1.5 liters of water, remove the dregs.

Directions　Fumigate and wash the anus with the decoction when it is warmly.

Indications　Hemorrhoids.

SECTION 6 Prolapse of Rectum

Recipe 1
Ingredients

  cimicifuga rhizome（*Rhizoma Cimicifugae*）
                                                 6 g
  cotton root   30 g
  hairy vein agrimony（*Herba Agrimoniae*）
                                                30 g
  Chinese angelica root（*Radix Angelicae Sinensis*）
                                                15 g
  astragalus root（*Radix astragali seu Hedysari*）
                                                15 g

Process   Decoct them in right amount of water and sift out the decoction from dregs.

Directions   Take it as drink, one dose daily.

Indications   Prolapse of rectum.

Recipe 2
Ingredients

  bark of Chinese – date tree   6 g

bark of pomegranate (*Pericarpium Granati*)

6 g

alum (*Alumen*)   4.5 g

Process   Decoct them in right amount of water until 300 ml of decoction left, let it warm.

Directions   Spread it on the affected part with a cotton dipped in the decoction.

Indications   Prolapse of rectum.

Recipe 3

Ingredients

lean pork   250 g

sea cucumber   30 g

Process   Soak the sea cucumber in water, cut the pork lean into cubes, decoct all them in right amount of water, season it with condiments.

Directions   Take it once a day. one administration consists of 3 – 5 days.

Indications   Prolapse of rectum.

SECTION 7 Angiitis

Recipe 1
Ingredients

poppy shell (Papaveris Capsulae)	60 g
aconite root (Radix Aconiti)	9 g
leech	9 g
parched earthworm (Lumbricus)	9 g
safflower (Flos Carthami)	15 g
millet wine	1250 ml

Process   Soak the first five ingredients in 1250 ml of water for 7 days, sift out the tincture from the dregs.

Directions   Take the tincture when one feel fain, 5 - 10 ml for each time.

Indications   Angiitis.

Recipe 2
Ingredients

prepared lateral root of aconite (Radix Aconiti Lateralis Praeparata)	9 g
cassia bark (Cortex Cinnamomi)	9 g

Chapter Two

    peach kernel (*Semen Persicae*)   9 g
    safflower (*Flos Carthami*)   9 g
    Chinese angelica root (*Radix Angelicae Sinensis*)
    9 g
    oriental water plantain rhizome (*Rhizoma Alismatis*)   9 g
    achyranthes root (*Radix Achyranthis Bidentatae*)
    9 g
    dried ginger (*Rhizoma Zingiberis*)   9 g
    Himalaya teasel root (*Radix Dipsaci*)   18 g
    scrophularia root (*Radix Scrophulariae*) 24 g
    crude astragalus root   24 g
    loranthus mulberry mistletoe (*Ramulus Loranthis*)   24 g
    spatholobus stem (*Caulis Spatholobi*)   24 g
    Chinese flowering quince (*Cydonia Lagenaria*)
    24 g
    cinnamon twig (*Ramulus Cinnamomi*)   24 g
    tetrandra root (*Radix Stephaniae Tetrandrae*)
    12 g
    red peony root (*Radix Paeoniae Rubra*) 12 g

Process   Decoct all them in right amount of water.

Directions   Take the decoction in twice and one dose for a day.

Indications   Angiitis.

Recipe 3

Ingredients

antler gelatin (*Colla Cornus Cervi*)	15 g
prepared rehmannia root (*Radix Rehmanniae Praeparata*)	50 g
cassia bark (*Cortex Cinnamomi*)	5 g
ephedra (*Herba Ephedrae*)	2 g
white mustard seed (*Semen Sinapis albae*)	10 g
carbonized ginger (*Zingiberis*)	2 g
liquorice (*Radix Glycyrrhizae*)	5 g

Process Decoct all them in right amount of water.

Directions Take it one dose daily.

Indications Angiitis.

Chapter Three
Gynecological and Obstetrical Diseases

SECTION 1 Dysmenorrhea

Recipe 1
Ingredients
 fresh milk   250 ml
 round - polished glutinous rice (*Semen Oryzae Sativae*)   60 g
 white sugar   right amount

Process Heat the rice and right amount of water in a pot over a strong fire, when it come to boil, heat it over a slow fire until it is done, add in the milk and sugar, go on cooking for a boil.

Directions Take it warmly, one dose daily.

Indications Dysmenorrhea.

Recipe 2

Ingredients

 red sage root (*Radix Salviae Miltiorrhizae*)

              100 g

 whitealcoholic drinks   500 g

Process Soak the red sage root in the spirit for about 20 days.

Directions Take right amount of it before menstruation.

Indications Dysmenorrhea.

Recipe 3

Ingredients

 aniseed (*Fructus Foeniculi*)   20 g
 Chinese angelica root (*Radix Angelicae Sinensis*)

              20 g

 Fruit of citron (*Fructus Aurantii*) 25 g
 powder of aniseed (*Fructus Foeniculi*) 10 g

Process Parch the aniseed until it smell sweat, then grind it into fine powder, decoct it with the Chinese angel root and fruit of the citron in right amount of water, sift out the decoction from the dregs. Infuse the powder with aniseed with the boiling decoction.

Directions Take it twice daily. Take 4 or 5 dose successively before the next menstruation.

Indications Dysmenorrhea.

Recipe 4
Ingredients

lychee - pit (*Semen Litchi*)	200 g
aniseed (*Fructus Foeniculi*)	10 g
sappan wood (*Lignum Sappan*)	200 g
spirit	500 ml

Process   Pound the stone of the litchi into pieces, then soak them with other ingredients in spirit for 20 days.

Directions   Take 5 ml each time before menstruation.

Indications   Dysmenorrhea.

Recipe 5
Ingredients

cyperus tuber (*Rhizoma Cyperi*)	15 g
Chinese angelica root (*Radix Angelicae Sinensis*)	15 g
corydalis tuber (*Rhizoma Corydalis*)	10 g
cassia bark (*Cortex Cinnamomi*)	6 g

Process   Decoct them in right amount of water.

Directions   Take the decoction in twice daily.

Indications   Dysmenorrhea.

Recipe 6
Ingredients

Chinese angelica root (*Radix Angelicae Sinensis*)	15 g

motherwort (*Herba Leonuri*) 15 g
red sage root (*Radix Salviae Miltiorrhizae*)
20 g
Chuanxiong Rhizome (*Rhizoma Ligustici Chuanxiong*) 6 g
asarum herb (*Herba Asari*) 5 g
white peony root (*Radix Paeoniae Alba*)
10 g
queen of the meadow (*Eupatorium*) 10 g
Corydalis tuber (*Radix Corydalis*) 10 g
Radix Linderae 10 g
dahurian Angelica root (*Radix Angelicae Dahuricae*) 10 g

Process   Decoct all them in right amount of water.

Directions   Take it a weeks before the menstruation, one dose daily for 3 successive courses. One course consists of 6 days.

Indications   Dysmenorrhea.

Recipe 7
Ingredients
rose (*Flos Rosae Rugosae*) 9 g
Chinese Rose (*Flos Rosae Chinensis*) 9 g
black tea 3 g

Process   Grind them into raw powder, then infuse them with boiling water and let stand for 10 minutes.

Directions Take it warmly, one dose daily for several days successively.

Indications Dysmenorrhea.

SECTION 2   Amenorrhea

Recipe 1
Ingredients
    Radix Salviae Miltiorrhizae   60 g
    brown sugar   60 g

Process   decoct them in right amount of water, then sift out the decoction from dregs.

Directions   Take it as drink both in the morning and in the evening.

Indications   Amenorrhea.

Recipe 2
Ingredients
    donkey – hide gelatin (*Colla Corii Asini*)
        30 g
    Semen Oryzae Sativae   50 g

Process   Stir – fry the donkey – hide gelatin in a pot until it is well done, dry it and grind it in fine powder. Make the rice into gruel, when it is nearly done, add in the fine powder of the donkey – hide gelatin in it and mix them well.

Directions   Take the gruel one dose daily for 7 days successively.

Indications   Amenorrhea.

Recipe 3
Ingredients

Juda's ear	50 g
sappan wood (*Lignum Sappan*)	50 g
millet wine	250 ml

Process   Decoct the first two ingredients in millet wine and half bowl of water until half bowl of decoction left.

Directions   Take right amount of it, twice or three times daily.

Indications   Amenorrhea.

Recipe 4
Ingredients

ginger (*Zingiberis*)	50 – 100 g
cuttlefish	400 g
cooking oil, *salt*	right amount for each

Process   Cut the ginger into thread, cut the cuttlefish into sections, and stir-fry the fish with the condiment in cooking oil.

Directions   Take the fish once daily. 7 successive days consisted of one course.

Indications   Amenorrhea.

SECTION 3 Irregular Menstruation

Recipe 1
Ingredients
    dangshen (*Radix Codonopsis Pilosulae*) 15 g
    astragalus root (*Radix astragali seu Hedysari*)
                                                       15 g
    Chinese angelica root (*Radix Angelicae Sinensis*)
                                                        10 g
    Chinese – date (*Fructus Ziziphi Jujubae*)
                                                        10 g
    liquorice (*Radix Glycyrrhizae*) 10 g
    red sage root (*Radix Salviae Miltiorrhizae*)
                                                        12 g
    cinnamon twig (*Ramulus Cinnamomi*) 5 g
    prepared rehmannia root (*Radix Rehmanniae Praeparata*) 30 g
    wheat (*Fructus Tritici*) 60 g
    longan (*Arillus Longan*) 20 g
    Chinese – date (*Fructus Ziziphi Jujubae*) 5
  Process Soak them in water for an hour, then ladle

them out and add in 1000 ml of water, decoct them over a slow fire, sift out the decoction, add in the wheat (Fructus Tritici), longan arial and Chinese-date in it, go on cooking to make gruel.

Directions　Take it twice daily.

Indications　Delayed menstruation due to blood insufficiency resulting from deficiency of spleen, postpartum fever, lochiorrhagia.

Recipe 2

Ingredients

　　ginseng（*Radix Ginseng*）　　　　　　6 g
　　dangshen（*Radix Codonopsis Pilosulae*）30 g
　　ginger（*Zingiberis*）　　　　　　　　5 slices
　　polished round-grained rice（*Semen Oryzae Sativae*）　　　　　　　　　　　　　　　100 g

Process　Make all them into gruel with right amount of water.

Directions　Take it twice or three times daily.

Indications　Advanced menstruation, spontaneous perspiration of deficiency type, prolapse of uterus. Contraindicated for cases with retention of heat evil.

Recipe 3

Ingredients

　　Chinese angelica root（*Radix Angelicae Sinensis*）

cyperus tuber (Rhizoma Cyperi)
Radix Linderae
motherwort fruit (Fructus Leonuri)
red peony root (Radix Paeoniae Rubra)
white peony root (Radix Paeoniae Alba)
rehmannia root (Radix Rehmanniae)
prepared rehmannia root (Radix Rehmanniae Praeparata)

Process   Decoct the above ingredients in water until it comes to boil.

Directions   Take the warm decoction one half in the morning and the remainder in the evening respectively. One dose daily. One course of treatment consists of 7 – 10 days.

Indications   Delayed menstruation.

Recipe 4
Ingredients

Himalaya teasel root (Radix Dipsaci)	30 g
Chinese angelica root (Radix Angelicae Sinensis)	30 g
oyster shell (Concha Ostreae)	30 g
epimedium (Herba Epimedii)	30 g
white peony root (Radix Paeoniae Alba)	20 g
psoralea fruit (Fructus Psoraleae)	20 g
fluorite (Lapis Fluoris)	20 g

Chuanxiong rhizome (Rhizoma Ligustici Chuanxiong)　　20 g
Corydalis tuber (Rhizoma Corydalis)　10 g
Radix Linderae　　10 g
liquorice (Radix Glycyrrhizae)　　10 g
dangshen (Radix Codonopsis Pilosulae)　15 g
hawthorn fruit (Fructus Crataegi)　　15 g

Process　Decoct all the ingredients in right amount of water.

Directions　Take 3 to 5 doses of the decoction in a week before the menstruation.

Indications　Aberratio mensium, dysplasia of the uterus, dysmenorrhea.

Recipe 5

Ingredients

peony (Flos Paeoniae)　　10 – 20 g
polished round – grained rice (Semen Oryzae Sativae)　　50 g
white sugar　　right amount

Process　Make the rice into gruel, when it come to one or two boils, add in the moutan flower, and go on cooking until it is well done, season it with sugar.

Directions　Take it before meals, twice daily.

Indications　Irregular menses, menorrhalgia.

Recipe 6

Ingredients

 longan pulp (*Arillus Longan*)   50 g
 egg   1

Process Decoct the longan in right amount of water for half an hour, beat the egg in it and go on cooking until it is well done.

Directions Take it twice daily.

Indications Irregular menses.

SECTION 4 Climacteric Syndrome

Recipe 1
Ingredients

Semen Oryzae Glutinosae	50 g
lucid ganoderma（Ganoderma Lucidum）	50 g
wheat（Fructus Tritici）	60 g
granulated sugar	30 g

Process   Wrap the lucid ganoderma with the gauze cloth, then put it and wheat and glutinous rice in an earthenware pot, add in one and a half bowl of water, heat them with a slow fire, when the glutinous wheat and wheat is well done, season it with crystal sugar.

Directions   Take it once daily.

Indications   Climacteric syndrome.

Recipe 2
Ingredients

lotus seed（Semen Nelumbinis）	50 g
longan（Arillus Longan）	50 g
jujube（Fructus Ziziphi Jujubae）	20 g

Semen Oryzae Glutinosae	100 g

Process   Make them into gruel with right amount of water in an earthenware pot.

Directions   Take it one dose daily.

Indications   Climacteric syndrome with scanty menses, pallor, lassitude and mental fatigue, etc..

Recipe 3
Ingredients

jellyfish	30 g
Bulbus Heleocharis Tuberosae	60 g
lotus seed	20 g
white sugar	right amount

Process   Decoct all the ingredients in right amount of water.

Directions   Take it one dose daily for 5 to 7 days successively.

Indications   Climacteric syndrome with psychic depression, irritability, anorexia, scanty menses, etc..

Recipe 4
Ingredients

wolfberry fruit（*Fructus Lycii*）	30 g
lily bulb（*Bulbus Lillii*）	60 g
egg	2
crystal sugar	right amount

Process　Decoct the wolfberry and lily bulb in the right amount of water, then remove the dregs, make a hole on the shell of egg, remove the egg white, take out the yolk and mix it with the decoction, season it with the crystal sugar.

Directions　Take it in twice, one dose daily.

Indications　Climacteric syndrome.

Recipe 5

Ingredients

  bupleurum root （*Radix Bupleuri*） 30 g
  white peony root （*Radix Paeoniae Alba*）
               30 g
  cyperus tuber （*Rhizoma Cyperi*） 30 g
  raw germinated barley （*Fructus Hordei Germinatus*） 30 g
  Chuanxiong Rhizome （*Rhizoma Ligustici Chuanxiong*） 10 g
  liquorice （*Radix Glycyrrhizae*） 10 g
  white sugar 250 g

Process　Decoct all the ingredients in 2 liters of water until 1.5 liters of decoction left, then remove the dregs by filtration. Season it with 250 g of sugar.

Directions　Take the solution twice or three times daily, 30 ml for each time.

Indications　Climacteric syndrome.

SECTION 5 Prolapse of Uterus

Recipe 1
Ingredients
  dangshen (*Radix Codonopsis Pilosulae*)   30 g
  cimicifuga rhizome (*Rhizoma Cimicifugae*)
                                              10 g
  millet crust   50 g

Process   Decoct the first two ingredients in right amount of water, remove the dregs, add in the millet crust and go on cooking to make a gruel.

Directions   Take it before meals twice daily.

Indications   Prolapse of uterus.

Recipe 2
Ingredients
  head of soft - shelled turtle   right amount
  millet wine   right amount

Process   Carbonize the head of soft - shell turtle over a fire, then grind it into fine powder.

Directions   Take the fine powder with the millet wine

three times daily, 6 g for each time.

Indications   Prolapse of uterus.

Recipe 3

Ingredients

Chicken's gizzard - membrane (*Endothelium Corneum Gigeriae Galli*)	4.5 g
lapis rubrum	9 g
gallnut	6 g
borneol (*Borneolum*)	0.6 g

Process   Grind all the ingredients into fine powder, seal them in a container for later use.

Directions   Take the powder three times daily.

Indications   Prolapse of uterus.

Recipe 4

Ingredients

ephedra (*Herba Ephedrae*)	6 g
aniseed (*Fructus Foeniculi*)	6 g
parched Fruit of citron (*Fructus Aurantii*)	1.2 g
gallnut	9 g

Process   Wrap all the ingredients with gauze cloth then soak it in warm water for 15 minutes, then heat it come to several boils.

Directions   Fumigate and wash the affect part with the

hot decoction, then push the uterus inward to its normal position.

Indications   Prolapse of uterus.

SECTION 6 Dysfunctional Uterine Bleeding

Recipe 1
Ingredients

cottonrose	15 g
Hindu lotus seedpod	20 g

Process   Decoct them in right amount of water, sift out the decoction.

Directions   Take it as drink, one dose daily.

Indications   Dysfunctional uterine bleeding.

Recipe 2
Ingredients

Hindu lotus seedpod
brown sugar

Process   Put Hindu lotus seedpod in an earthenware pot, roast it over fire until it becomes burnt yellow in color. Grind it into powder. Wrap it in a piece of gauze, put it along with brown sugar in the cup, add in boiled water.

Directions   Take the warm drink instead of tea.

Indications   Menorrhagia.

Recipe 3

Ingredients

longan (*Arillus Longan*)	30 g
lotus seed (*Semen Nelumbinis*)	30 g
Chinese - date (*Fructus Ziziphi Jujubae*)	10 g
polished glutinous rice (*Semen Oryzae Glutinosae*)	60 g
white sugar	right amount

Process　Remove the stone of the Chinese - date and clean up the glutinous rice. heat the Chinese - date, longan arial and lotus seed, glutinous rice and right amount of water over a strong fire, when it come to boil, go on heat it over a slow fire until it is well done. Season it with sugar.

Directions　Take it one dose daily.

Indications　Mild chronic vaginal bloody discharge.

Recipe 4

Ingredients

red phaseolus bean (*Semen Phaseoli*)	30 g
astragalus root (*Radix astragali seu Hedysari*)	30 g
longan pulp (*Arillus Longan*)	7
jujube (*Fructus Ziziphi Jujubae*)	7

Process　Decoct all them in right amount of water.

Directions　Take the decoction twice daily, both in the morning and in the evening.

Indications　Dysfunctional uterine bleeding, especially menorrhagia.

Recipe 5

Ingredients

　　donkey－hide gelatin（*Colla Corii Asini*）
　　　　　　　　　　　　　　　　　　　　30 g

　　polished glutinous rice（*Semen Oryzae Glutinosae*）　　　　　　　　　　　　　　100 g

　　brown sugar　　　　　　　　right amount

Process　Make the rice into gruel, when the gruel is nearly done, add in the pounded donkey－hide gelatin and go on cooking with stir, when it come to two or three boils, add in the brown sugar.

Directions　Take it in twice daily.

Indications　Dysfunctional uterine bleeding, and other hemorrhages such as epistaxis, hematemesis, hematochezia, etc. due to blood insufficiency.

Recipe 6

Ingredients

　　dangshen（*Radix Codonopsis Pilosulae*）　9 g
　　parched white atractylodes rhizome（*Rhizoma Atractylodis Macrocephalae*）　　　　　　　9 g

parched Chinese-date (*Fructus Ziziphi Jujubae*) 9 g
Himalaya teasel root (*Radix Dipsaci*) 9 g
tangerine peel (*Pericarpium Citri Reticulatae*) 9 g
ginger (*Zingiberis*) 9 g
astragalus root (*Radix astragali seu Hedysari*) 12 g
motherwort (*Herba Leonuri*) 12 g
donkey-hide gelatin (*Colla Corii Asini*) 12 g
oyster shell (*Concha Ostreae*) 15 g
prepared liquorice (*Radix Glycyrrhizae Praeparata*) 3 g
aucklandia root (*Radix Aucklandiae*) 3 g

Process Decoct all the ingredients in right amount of water.

Directions Take it in twice, one dose daily.

Indications Dysfunctional uterine bleeding.

SECTION 7　Habitual Abortion

Recipe 1

Ingredients

ginseng (*Radix Ginseng*)	15 g
astragalus root (*Radix astragali seu Hedysari*)	30 g
rehmannia root (*Radix Rehmanniae*)	20 g
donkey-hide gelatin (*Colla Corii Asini*)	30 g
white honey	100 ml

Process　Decoct the first ingredients in 500 ml of water for twice, sift out the decoctions. Put the decoctions together and enrich it until 300 ml of decoction left. Put the donkey-hide gelatin and 100 ml of water in a bowl, then steam it over water in a steamer until the donkey-hide gelatin it melt. Mix the it with the decoction and add in the honey to get jelly.

Directions　Take it three times daily, 20 ml each time, and one course consists of the 30 days.

Indications　Habitual abortion.

Surgical Diseases

Recipe 2

Ingredients

donkey-hide gelatin (*Colla Corii Asini*)
             10 g

egg   1

Process Dissolve the donkey-hide gelatin in 250 ml warm water, stir the egg in the solution, heat it until the water comes to boil. Then season it with salt.

Directions Take it one or two dose a day.

Indications Habitual abortion.

Recipe 3

Ingredients

Semen Oryzae Glutinosae	30 g
Radix astragali seu Hedysari	15 g
Rhizoma Ligustici Chuanxiong	5 g

Process Decoct all the ingredients in 1000 ml of water, when the 500 ml decoction left, sift out the decoction from dregs.

Directions Take the decoction in twice.

Indications Habitual abortion.

Recipe 4

Ingredients

Caulis Perillae Acutae	9 g
amomum fruit (*Fructus Amomi*)	5 g
lotus seed (*Semen Nelumbinis*)	60 g

Process   Get rid of the peel and pith, put it in a jar and add in 500 ml of water, steam it over water in a steam, when it is 90 per cent done, add in the other ingredients and 500 ml of water, go on heat it over a slow fire until the lotus seed well done.

Directions   Eat the lotus seed and drink the soup. Take it once or twice daily.

Indications   Habitual abortion.

Recipe 5
Ingredients

ginseng (*Radix Ginseng*)	60 g
poria (*Poria*)	60 g
prepared liquorice (*Radix Glycyrrhizae Praeparata*)	60 g
Chinese angelica root (*Radix Angelicae Sinensis*)	60 g
donkey - hide gelatin (*Colla Corii Asini*)	60 g
silkworm cocoon (*Coccum Bombycis*)	60 g
cuttle bone	60 g

parched Himalaya teasel root (Radix Dipsaci)
60 g
white atractylodes rhizome (Rhizoma Atractylodis Macrocephalae) 300 g
astragalus root (Radix astragali seu Hedysari)
180 g
prepared rehmannia root (Radix Rehmanniae Praeparata) 90 g
dogwood fruit (Fructus Corni) 90 g
eucommia bark (Cortex Eucommiae) 90 g
dodder seed (Semen Cuscutae) 90 g
capejasmine fruit (Fructus Gardeniae) 90 g
Chinese yam (Rhizoma Dioscoreae) 90 g
scutellaria root (Radix Scutellariae) 240 g
loranthus mulberry mistletoe (Ramulus Loranthis) 120 g
jujube (Fructus Ziziphi Jujubae) 1000 g

Process Grind the first eighteen ingredients into fine powder, then stew the Chinese-date in water, when it is done, remove the peel and stone of it, then pound it into mash, make it with other ingredients into boluses.

Directions Take it with boiled water, both in the morning and in the evening, 6 g for each time.

Indications Habitual abortion.

SECTION 8 Sterility

Recipe 1
Ingredients

　　bupleurum root (Radix Bupleuri)　　　　6 g
　　white peony root (Radix Paeoniae Alba)
　　　　　　　　　　　　　　　　　　　10 g
　　red peony root (Radix Paeoniae Rubra)　10 g
　　queen of the meadow　　　　　　　　10 g
　　motherwort (Herba Leonuri)　　　　　10 g
　　spatholobus stem (Caulis Spatholobi)　　10 g
　　achyranthes root (Radix Achyranthis Bidentatae)
　　　　　　　　　　　　　　　　　　　10 g
　　sappan wood (Lignum Sappan)　　　　10 g
　　cat－tail pollen (Pollen Typhae)　　　10 g
　　glossy privet fruit (Fructus Ligustri Lucidi)
　　　　　　　　　　　　　　　　　　　10 g
　　raspberry (Fructus Rubi)　　　　　　10 g
　　dodder seed (Semen Cuscutae)　　　　10 g
　　wolfberry fruit (Fructus Lycii)　　　　10 g

Process　Decoct all the ingredients in right amount of

water.

Directions   Take 6 – 9 doses every month. Take the first 3 – 4 doses during the menstrual period, one dose daily. The other 3 – 5 doses are taken from the 13th day of the mentruation, once daily.

Indications   Sterility due to dysovarism.

Recipe 2
Ingredients
  red sage root (*Radix Salviae Miltiorrhizae*)
                                                                    12 g
  peach kernel (*Semen Persicae*)   9 – 12 g
  red peony root (*Radix Paeoniae Rubra*)
                                                                9 – 12 g
  Corydalis tuber (*Radix Corydalis*)   9 – 12 g
  Chinese angelica root (*Radix Angelicae Sinensis*)
                                                                      9 g
  safflower (*Flos Carthami*)   9 g
  Radix Bupleuri   9 g
  Fructus Meliae Toosendan   9 g
    Chuanxiong Rhizome (*Rhizoma Ligustici Chuanxiong*)   6 g
    aniseed (*Fructus Foeniculi*)   6 g

Process   decoct all the ingredients in right amount of the water.

Directions   Take the decoction.

Indications　Sterility.

Recipe 3
Ingredients

　　red sage root（*Radix Salviae Miltiorrhizae*）
　　　　　　　　　　　　　　　　20 g
　　poria（*Poria*）　　　　　　　15 g
　　bupleurum root（*Radix Bupleuri*）　10 g
　　Immature bitter orange（*Fructus Aurantii Immaturus*）　　　　　　　　　　10 g
　　red peony root（*Radix Paeoniae Rubra*）10 g
　　pueraria root（*Radix Puerariae*）　10 g
　　liquorice（*Radix Glycyrrhizae*）　　3 g

Process　Decoct them in right amount of water for 15 minutes, then sift out the decoction from dregs, add right amount of water in the dregs, and go on cooking for 20 minutes, then sift out the decoction. Put the decoctions together and mix them well.

Directions　Take one dose daily. Take five doses before the menstruation.

Indications　Sterility.

SECTION 9 Leukorrhagia

Recipe 1
Ingredients
Rhizoma et Radix Baphicacanthis   20 g
jujube (*Fructus Ziziphi Jujubae*)   10 g

Process   Cut all them into pieces and decoct them into right amount of water.

Directions   Take the decoction as drink, one dose daily.

Indications   Leukorrhagia.

Recipe 2
Ingredients
white hyacinth bean (*Semen Dolichoris*) 20 g
Chinese yam (*Rhizoma Dioscoreae*)   20 g
white sugar   right amount

Process   Parch the white hyacinth bean until it become yellow, then pound it into pieces. Cut the Chinese yam into slices, then decoct them with the white hyacinth bean in right amount of water. When it is done, sift out the decoction, and dissolve the sugar in it.

Directions　Take it as drink.

Indications　Leukorrhagia.

Recipe 3

Ingredients

waxgourd (*Fructus Benincasae*)　　　50 g

ginkgo nut (*Semen Ginkgo*)　　　10 stains

Process　Decoct them in one and a half bowls of water until half bowl of decoction left.

Directions　Take it twice daily.

Indications　Leukorrhagia.

Recipe 4

Ingredients

lotus seed (*Semen Nelumbinis*)　　　100 g

euryal seed (*Semen Euryales*)　　　100 g

fresh lotus leaf (*Folium Nelumbinis*)　　50 g

polished glutinous rice (*Semen Oryzae Glutinosae*)　　　50 g

granulated sugar　　　right amount

Process　Make the first four ingredients into gruel with right amount of water. Then season it with crystal sugar.

Directions　Take the gruel.

Indications　Leukorrhagia.

Recipe 5

Ingredients

fresh lotus rhizome（*Rhizoma Nelumbinis*）
100 g
common cockscomb（*Flos Celosiae Cristatae*）
3

Process　Cut the lotus root into threads, wrap then with gauze cloth and extract it juice, decoct it and common cockscomb in right amount of water for 20 minutes, sift out the decoction. Season it with the sugar.

Directions　Take it twice daily, 50 – 100 ml for each time.

Indications　Leukorrhagia.

Recipe 6

Ingredients

white atractylodes rhizome（*Rhizoma Atractylodis Macrocephalae*）	250 g
Chinese yam（*Rhizoma Dioscoreae*）	250 g
peanut（*Arachis Hypogaea*）	250 g
brown sugar	200 g

Process　parch the first ingredients into rill, then grind them into fine powder, mix them with brown sugar well.

Directions　Take it three times daily, 30 g for each time.

Indications　Leukorrhagia.

SECTION 10 Vomiting During Pregnancy

Recipe 1

Ingredients

ophiopogon root（*Radix Ophiopogonis*） 10 g
stem of purple perilla（*Caulis Perillae Acutae*） 10 g
scrophularia root（*Radix Scrophulariae*）18 g
bamboo shaving（*Caulis Bambusae in Taeniam*） 6 g
coptis（*Rhizoma Coptidis*） 3 g
black plum（*Fructus Nume*） 2
parched scutellaria root（*Radix Scutellariae*） 5 g

Process Soak all the ingredients in right amount of water, then decoct them for 30 minutes, sift out the decoction from dregs, repeat this process again. Put the decoctions together.

Directions Take the decoction in twice daily, both in the morning and in the evening.

Indications Vomiting during pregnancy.

Recipe 2

Ingredients

agastache（*Herba Pogostemonis seu Agastachis*）	9 g
dried orange peel（*Pericarpium Citri*）	6 g
pinellia tuber（*Rhizoma Pinelliae*）	6 g
stem of purple perilla（*Caulis Perillae Acutae*）	6 g
amomum fruit（*Fructus Amomi*）	3 g

Process Soak the first four ingredients in water for 30 minutes, then decoct them in right amount of water for 30 minutes, twice, sift out the decoctions from dregs, then put the decoctions together.

Directions Take it in twice daily, both in the morning and in the evening.

Indications Vomiting during pregnancy.

Recipe 3

Ingredients

Humus Flava Usta	50 g
tick clover	50 g
ginger（*Zingiberis*）	25 g

Process Decoct the baked yellow earth in 1000 ml water in a pot, sift out the decoction from dregs, then add the other ingredients it the decoction and go on cooking, sift out the decoction from dregs.

Directions Take it as drink.

Indications Vomiting during pregnancy.

Recipe 4

Ingredients

purple perilla leaves (*Folium Perillae*) 4.5 g

ginger juice (*Succus Zingiberis*) *a few drops*

Process Tear the purple perilla leaves into pieces, then infuse it with juice of the ginger with boiling water.

Directions Take it as drink.

Indications Vomiting during pregnancy.

Recipe 5

Ingredients

ginseng (*Radix Ginseng*)	15 g
pinellia tuber (*Rhizoma Pinelliae*)	15 g
dried ginger (*Rhizoma Zingiberis*)	5 g
ginger juice (*Succus Zingiberis*)	10 ml
juice of rehmannia root (*Succus Radicis Rehmanniae*)	30 ml
wheat (*Fructus Tritici*)	right amount

Process Mix all the ingredients well to make it into small 10 cakes, then steam them over water in a steamer.

Directions Take it twice or three times daily, 2 for each time.

Surgical Diseases

Indications   Vomiting during pregnancy.

Recipe 6
Ingredients
   olive   right amount

Process   Clean it up and pound it into mash, then decoct it in right amount of water.

Directions   Take it twice or three times daily.

Indications   Vomiting during pregnancy.

SECTION 11 Edema During Pregnancy

Recipe 1
Ingredients

black soybean	50 g
longan (*Arillus Longan*)	15 g
jujube (*Fructus Ziziphi Jujubae*)	50 g

Process Decoct all the ingredients in right amount of water.

Directions Take it in twice daily, both in the morning and in the evening.

Indications Edema during pregnancy.

Recipe 2
Ingredients

carp	400 g
red phaseolus bean (*Semen Phaseoli*)	200 g
dried orange peel (*Pericarpium Citri*)	10 g
garlic (*Bulbus Allii*)	1

Process Get rid of the scales, and entrails, decoct all the ingredients in right amount of water until it is well done.

Surgical Diseases

Directions　Eat the carp and drink the soup, take it in three times.

Indications　Edema during pregnancy.

SECTION 12　Lack of Lactation

Recipe 1
Ingredients
　　astragalus root（*Radix astragali seu Hedysari*）
　　　　　　　　　　　　　　　　　　40 g
　　dangshen（*Radix Codonopsis Pilosulae*）30 g
　　ophiopogon root（*Radix Ophiopogonis*）15 g
　　rehmannia root（*Radix Rehmanniae*）　15 g
　　Chinese angelica root（*Radix Angelicae Sinensis*）
　　　　　　　　　　　　　　　　　　15 g
　　platycodon root（*Radix Platycodi*）　　10 g
　　manshurian aristolochia stem（*Caulis Aristolochae Manshuriensis*）　　10 g
　　parched vaccaria seed（*Semen Vaccariae*）
　　　　　　　　　　　　　　　　　　10 g
　　pangolin scales（*Squama Manitis*）　　　6 g
　　ricepaper pith（*Medulla Terrapanacis*）　6 g
　　Chinese honeylocust spine（*Spina Gleditsiae*）
　　　　　　　　　　　　　　　　　　6 g
　　trichosanthes root（*Radix Trichosanthis*）6 g

Surgical Diseases

  globethistle root   6 g
  brown sugar   right amount
  porcine trotters one pair

 Process Grind the first thirteen ingredients into fine powder, then decoct the pig's foot in right amount of water until it is well done, remove the float oil and infuse the fine powder with it.

 Directions Take it once daily.

 Indications Lack of lactation.

Recipe 2

Ingredients

  peach kernel (*Semen Persicae*)

  polished round-grained rice (*Semen Oryzae Sativae*)

  brown sugar

 Process Decoct the first two ingredients in a right amount of water to make gruel. After it is done, add in right amount of brown sugar.

 Directions Take the gruel once daily.

 Indications Lack of lactation and postpartum fever.

Recipe 3

Ingredients

  pangolin scales (*Squama Manitis*)   15 g

Chapter Two

Chinese angelica root (*Radix Angelicae Sinensis*)
　　　　　　　　　　　　　　　　　　　　10 g
old hen　　　　　　　　　　　　　　　　　1

Process　Wrap the Chinese angel root and pangolin scales with the gauze cloth, then decoct it with the hen in right amount of water until the hen is well done.

Directions　Eat the meat and drink the soup.

Indications　Lack of lactation due to deficiency of qi and blood.

Recipe 4
Ingredients
　　day lily (*Flos Hemerocallis*)　　　　50 g
　　lean pork　　　　　　　　　　　　200 g
　　salt　　　　　　　　　　　　right amount

Process　Stew the daylily and pork lean in right amount of water, then season it with right amount of salt.

Directions　Take it with other foods.

Indications　Lack of lactation.

Recipe 5
Ingredients
　　lettuce seed　　　　　　　　　　10 – 15 g
　　liquorice (*Radix Glycyrrhizae*)　　　3 – 5 g
　　polished round – grained rice (*Semen Oryzae Sativae*)　　　　　　　　　　　　　　　100 g

Surgical Diseases

Process　Pound the lettuce seed into pieces, then decoct them with the liquorice in right amount of water, remove the dregs, then add in the rice and go on cooking to make a thin gruel.

Directions　Take it three times daily, one course consists of the 3 to 5 days.

Indications　Lack of lactation.

SECTION 13　Recipes for Delactation

Recipe 1
Ingredients
　　fermented soy bean　　　　　　　　30 g
　　orchid drunk　　　　　　　　　　30 ml
　Process　Pound the prepare soya bean into pieces, then make it into paste with the spirit.
　Directions　Spread it on the chest and keep it moisten.
　Indications　Used for delactation.

Recipe 2
Ingredients
　　germinated barley (*Fructus Hordei Germinatus*)
　　　　　　　　　　　　　　　　　　30 g
　　achyranthes root (*Radix Achyranthis Bidentatae*)
　　　　　　　　　　　　　　　　　　9 g
　　red peony root (*Radix Paeoniae Rubra*)　9 g
　　peach kernel (*Semen Persicae*)　　　6 g
　　safflower (*Flos Carthami*)　　　　　6 g
　　queen of the meadow　　　　　　　6 g

Chinese angelica root (Radix Angelicae Sinensis)
6 g
Chuanxiong Rhizome (Rhizoma Ligustici Chuanxiong) 3 g

Process   Decoct all the ingredients in right amount of water.

Directions   Take it in twice daily.

Indications   Used for delactation.

Recipe 3

Ingredients

Rhizoma Arisaema cum Bile Praeparata   10 g

Process   Grind it into fine powder, then make it into paste with vinegar.

Directions   Spread it over the chest, keep it over one day.

Indications   Used for delactation.

Chapter Four Pediatric Diseases

SECTION 1 Common Cold in Children

Recipe 1
Ingredients
    tomato juice   right amount
    water melon juice   right amount
Process   Mix the juices together.
Directions   Take it as drink.
Indications   Common cold in children.

Recipe 2
Ingredients
    fresh olive   30 g
    radish (*Napus*)   250 g
Process   Clean the radish up and cut it into slices, then decoct them with the olive in right amount of water, sift out the decoction from dregs.

Pediatric Diseases

Directions Take the decoction as drink.
Indications Common cold in children.

SECTION 2　Cough and Asthma in Children

Recipe 1

Ingredients

fresh lily bulb (*Bulbus Lillii*)	50 g
polished glutinous rice (*Semen Oryzae Glutinosae*)	50 g
crystal sugar	right amount

Process　Make the gelatin rice and lily bulb into gruel with right amount of water, when it is done, add in the crystal sugar and mix them well.

Directions　Take it warmly.

Indications　Cough, shortness of breath, choking cough due to excessive sputum, anorexia, etc..

Recipe 2

Ingredients

chestnut	50 g
corn stigma (*Stigma Maydis*)	10 g
crystal sugar	50 g

Process　Decoct all the ingredients in one bowl of water

in a pot over a slow fire until half bowl of decoction left.

Directions   Take it at once time.

Indications   Prolonged cough, asthma.

Recipe 3

Ingredients

fresh lotus root (*Rhizoma Nelumbinis*)

250 g

honey (*Mel*)   50 g

Process   Add the honey in the juice of the lotus root.

Directions   Take it in five times for several days.

Indications   Cough due to lung – heat retention, dry and sore throat, nosebleed due to blood – heat evil.

SECTION 3 Whooping Cough

Recipe 4
Ingredients

    Sichuan fritillary bulb (*Bulb Fritillariae Cirrhosae*)　　9 g
    crystal sugar　　15 g
    millet soup　　150 – 200 g

Process　Heat the rice in right amount of water, when it come to boil, sift out the decoction, add the crystal sugar and Sichuan fritillary bulb in the decoction and steam them over water in a steamer until they are well done.

Directions　Take it twice daily, both in the morning and in the evening.

Indications　Whooping cough.

Recipe 5
Ingredients
    pear (*Malum Piri*)　　1
    ephedra (*Herba Ephedrae*)　　0.5 g

Process　Clean the pear up and remove its stone, then

Pediatric Diseases

put the ephedra in the hole of the pear, then steam it over water in a steam. When it is done, remove the ephedra.

Directions   Eat the pear and drink the juice. Take it in twice daily.

Indications   Whooping cough.

Recipe 6
Ingredients

crystal sugar	500 g
peanut	250 g

Process   First decoct crystal sugar in a small amount of water over a slow fire until the crystal sugar becomes colloid with little glutinosity. Add in stir-fried peanuts and mix them well. Press the mixture into plane and cut it into pieces for later use.

Directions   Take the mixture frequently.

Indications   Whooping cough.

SECTION 4　Morbilli Measles

Recipe 1
Ingredients
　　cane（*Saccharum Officinarum*）　　　100 g
　　water chestnut（*Bulbus Heleocharis Tuberosae*）
　　　　　　　　　　　　　　　　　　100 g
　　Radish（*Napus*）　　　　　　　　100 g
Process　Clean them up and cut them into small cubes, then decoct them in 500 ml of water over a slow fire until 250 decoction left.
Directions　Take the decoction as drink.
Indications　Measles.

Recipe 2
Ingredients
　　cicada slough（*Periostracum Cicadae*）　3 g
Process　Decoct it in right amount of water.
Directions　Take it in several times daily.
Indications　Measles.

Recipe 3
Ingredients

olive seed   500 g

Process   Let the olive stone dry, and pound it into fine powder, then mix it with flour and right amount of water to make small cakes.

Directions   Take it as staple food.

Indications   Measles. Can also prevent the occurrence of measles.

Recipe 4
INGREDIENT: mutton   50 g

coriander (*Herba Coriandri*)   50 g

spirit   right amount

Process   Decoct the mutton, coriander and a few drops of spirit in right amount of water for an hour.

Directions   Take it twice daily.

Indications   Measles.

Recipe 5
Ingredients

fresh mushroom   250 g

crucian carp   1

salt   right amount

Process   Kill the carp and remove its entrails, then decoct it with the mushroom in right amount of water until the decoction is white, then season it with salt.

    Directions   Eat the fish and drink the soup.

    Indications   Measles.

SECTION 5 Varicella

Recipe 1
Ingredients

lily bulb（*Bulbus Lillii*）	10 g
apricot kernel（*Semen Armeniacae*）	6 g
red phaseolus bean（*Semen Phaseoli*）	60 g

Process   Decoct all the ingredients in right amount of water to get a thick decoction.

Directions   Take it in any time.

Indications   Varicella.

Recipe 2
Ingredients

fresh coriander（*Herba Coriandri*）	150 g
Radish（*Napus*）	200 g
chestnut	150 g
fresh water chestnut（*Bulbus Heleocharis Tuberosae*）	150 g

Process   Clean all them up and cut them into pieces, then decoct all them in right amount of water, sift out 800 ml of decoction from the dregs.

    Directions   Take it in twice, one dose daily.

    Indications   Varicella.

    Recipe 3

    Ingredients

    tendril − leave fritillary bulb (*Bulbus Fritillariae Cirrhosae*)   6 g

    apricot kernel (*Semen Armeniacae*)   3 g

    honey (*Mel*)   right amount

Process   Decoct the apricot kernel and Sichuan fritillary bulb in right amount of water.

Directions   Take it two or three times daily. Season it with honey before eat.

Indications   Varicella.

SECTION 6　Parotitis

Recipe 1
Ingredients
　wild chrysanthemum flower（*Flos Chrysanthemi*）
　　　　　　　　　　　　　　　　　　39 g
　Sophora Subprostrata　　　　　　10 g
　dandelion herb（*Herba Taraxaci*）　30 g
Process　Decoct all the ingredients in right amount of water, sift out the decoction from dregs.
Directions　Take it as drink, one dose daily.
Indications　Mumps.

Recipe 2
Ingredients
　isatis root（*Radix Isatidis*）　　　30 g
　honeysuckle flower（*Flos Lonicerae*）　10 g
　peppermint（*Herba Menthae*）　　5 g
Process　Grind all them into raw powder, then decoct them in right amount of water, sift out the decoction from dregs.

Directions　Take it as drink.
Indications　Mumps.

Recipe 3
Ingredients
　　fresh day lily root　　　　　　　　60 g
　　crystal sugar　　　　　　　　right amount
Process　Decoct all the ingredients in right amount of water over a slow fire for 30 minutes.

Directions　Take it in twice daily, one dose daily for 3 to 5 doses successively.

Indications　Mumps.

Recipe 4
Ingredients
　　isatis root (*Radix Isatidis*)　　　　30 g
　　prunella spike (*Spica Prunellae*)　　20 g
　　white sugar　　　　　　　　right amount

Pediatric Diseases

Process　Decoct the first ingredients in right amount of water, then add in right amount of sugar.

Directions　Take it three times daily, 10 – 20 g for each time.

Indications　Mumps.

SECTION 7   Anorexia

Recipe 1

Ingredients

　　medicated leaven (*Massa Fermentata Medicinalis*)
　　　　　　　　　　　　　　　　15 g

　　parched germinated barley (*Fructus Hordei Germinatus*)　　　　　　　　　　15 g

　　carbonized hawthorn fruit (*Fructus Crataegi*)
　　　　　　　　　　　　　　　　15 g

　　areca seed (*Semen Arecae*)　　　　9 g

　　dried orange peel (*Pericarpium Citri*)　　6 g

　　aucklandia root (*Radix Aucklandiae*)　　6 g

　　prepared liquorice (*Radix Glycyrrhizae Praeparata*)　　　　　　　　　　　　　　4.5 g

Process   Decoct all the ingredients twice, sift out the decoction then mix them well.

Directions   Take it in twice.

Indications   Anorexia.

Recipe 2

Pediatric Diseases

Ingredients

    white atractylodes rhizome（*Rhizoma Atractylodis Macrocephalae*） 6 g
    hawthorn fruit（*Fructus Crataegi*） 6 g
    germinated barley（*Fructus Hordei Germinatus*）
        6 g
    rice sprout（*Fructus Oryzae Germinatus*） 6 g
    medicated leaven（*Massa Fermentata Medicinalis*）
        6 g
    Immature bitter orange（*Fructus Aurantii Immaturus*） 6 g
    dried orange peel（*Pericarpium Citri*） 6 g
    atractylodes rhizome（*Rhizoma Atractylodis*）
        6 g
    dendrobium（*Herba Dendrobii*） 6 g
    astragalus root（*Radix astragali seu Hedysari*）
        6 g

Process Soak all the ingredients in right amount of water for 20 minutes, then decoct them for 15 minutes, sift out the decoction from dregs, add right amount of water in the dregs, decoct them for 20 minutes, then sift out the decoction, mix the decoctions well.

Directions Take it in twice, one dose daily.

Indications Anorexia..

Recipe 3

Chapter Four

Ingredients

    amomum fruit (*Fructus Amomi*)   2 - 3 g

    aucklandia root (*Radix Aucklandiae*) 1 - 2 g

    lotus rhizome (*Rhizoma Nelumbinis*)

                                  30 - 50 g

    white sugar   right amount

Process   Grind the aucklandia root and amomum fruit into fine powder, then mix 1/5 - 1/3 of the powder with lotus root and sugar, then soak the mixture with boiled water. Churn the mixture to make gruel.

Directions   Take it once or twice every day along with staple food. One course consists of three days of treatment.

Indications   Anorexia.

Recipe 4

Ingredients

    germinated barley (*Fructus Hordei Germinatus*)

                                  120 g

    tangerine peel (*Pericarpium Citri Reticulatae*)

                                  30 g

    parched white atractylodes rhizome (*Rhizoma Atractylodis Macrocephalae*)   30 g

    medicated leaven (*Massa Fermentata Medicinalis*)

                                  60 g

    ground rice   150 g

    white sugar   right amount

Pediatric Diseases

Process　Wash germinated barley clean and dry them along with fresh tangerine peel in the sun. Grind the first four ingredients into powder. Mix it with sugar and ground rice. Add water in the mixture to make small cakes. Then steam the cakes over fire until they are done.

Directions　Eat 2 or 3 cakes a day. One course of treatment consists of 5 − 7 days.

Indications　Poor appetite with fullness sensation of the abdomen.

Recipe 5
Ingredients

areca seed (*Semen Arecae*)　　　　　　5 − 10 g
Radish seed (*Semen Napus*)　　　　　　5 − 10 g
fresh tangerine peel (*Pericarpium Citri Reticulatae*)　　　　　　　　　　　　　　　10 − 15 g
white sugar　　　　　　　　　　right amount

Process　Pound he areca seed into pieces, Parch the radish seed in a pot until it smell well, then take a fresh orange peel and cut it into threads, decoct the first ingredients in right amount of water for 5 − 7 minutes, then sift out the decoction from dregs, season the decoction with right amount of water.

Directions　Take it in twice or three times daily, one dose daily.

Indications　Anorexia.

Chapter Four

SECTION 8   Infantile Malnutrition

Recipe 1
Ingredients

glove (*Flos Caryophylli*)	2 stains
ginger juice (*Succus Zingiberis*)	a spoon
milk	250 ml
white sugar	right amount

Process   Decoct the glove, juice of ginger and milk in a pot, when it come to boil, remove the glove and add in the sugar.

Directions   Take it warmly, both in the morning and in the evening.

Indications   Infantile malnutrition.

Recipe 2
Ingredients

ginseng (*Radix Ginseng*)	6 g
white poria (*Poria*)	10 g
ophiopogon root (*Radix Ophiopogonis*)	10 g
Semen Oryzae Sativae	50 g

Process　Decoct the ginseng in right amount of water over a slow fire for 30 minutes, then add in the white poria and ophiopogon root, go on cooking over a slow fire for 30 minutes, sift out the decoction from dregs. Make a gruel with the rice and right amount of water, when it is nearly done, add in the decoction, and go on cooking for a while.

Directions　Take it as dinner.

Indications　Infantile malnutrition.

Recipe 3

Ingredients

frog	500 g
dangshen (*Radix Codonopsis Pilosulae*)	60 g
Chinese yam (*Rhizoma Dioscoreae*)	30 g
jujube (*Fructus Ziziphi Jujubae*)	10 g
salt	right amount

Process　Kill the frogs and remove the skins, internal organs and heads, wash them clean. Decoct them along with Chinese yam in a right amount of water over a strong fire until it comes to boil. Then decoct them over a slow fire for one to two hours. Season the decoction with salt after it is done.

Directions　Take the decoction along with staple food.

Indications　Infantile malnutrition with general deficiency, thin build, fullness of the abdomen, poor appetite, restlessness, difficulty in sleeping calmly, fever of deficiency type.

SECTION 9 Diarrhea in Children

Recipe 1
Ingredients
　　black plum (*Fructus Nume*)　　　　　2 g
　　Fructus Chebulae　　　　　　　　　　3 g
Process　Infuse them with boiling water.
Directions　Take it warmly five to six times daily.
Indications　Diarrhea.

Recipe 2
Ingredients
　　white atractylodes rhizome (*Rhizoma Atractylodis Macrocephalae*)　　　　　　　　　　　3 g
　　dangshen (*Radix Codonopsis Pilosulae*)　3 g
　　pueraria root (*Radix Puerariae*)　　　3 g
　　Poria　　　　　　　　　　　　　　　3 g
　　ophiopogon root (*Radix Ophiopogonis*)　9 g
　　aucklandia root (*Radix Aucklandiae*)　0.9 g
　　prepared liquorice (*Radix Glycyrrhizae Praeparata*)　　　　　　　　　　　　　　　　1.5 g

　　　　agastache (*Herba Pogostemonis seu Agastachis*)
　　　　　　　　　　　　　　　　　　　　1.5 g
　　　Chinese – date (*Fructus Ziziphi Jujubae*)　　1
　　　　ginger (*Zingiberis*)　　　　　　　1 slice

　　Process　Decoct all the ingredients in right amount of water.

　　Directions　Take it as drink, one dose daily.

　　Indications　Diarrhea.

Recipe 3

Ingredients

　　　Chinese yam (*Rhizoma Dioscoreae*)　　100 g
　　　lotus root (*Rhizoma Nelumbinis*)　　　100 g
　　　germinated barley (*Fructus Hordei Germinatus*)
　　　　　　　　　　　　　　　　　　　　50 g
　　　poria (*Poria*)　　　　　　　　　　　50 g
　　　round – polished glutinous rice (*Semen Oryzae Sativae*)　　　　　　　　　　　　　　500 g
　　　white sugar　　　　　　　　　　　100 g

　　Process　Grind the first five ingredients into fine powder, then make them into paste with right amount of water. Season it with sugar.

　　Directions　Take it three times daily.

　　Indications　Diarrhea.

Recipe 4

Ingredients

    white hyacinth bean（*Semen Dolichoris*） 15 g
    ginseng（*Radix Ginseng*）   5 – 10 g
    polished round – grained rice（*Semen Oryzae Sativae*）   50 g

Process Stew the white hyacinth bean in right amount of water, when it is nearly done, add in rice and go on cooking to make a gruel. Decoct the ginseng in right amount of water and sift out the decoction from dregs. When the gruel is nearly done, add in the decoction of ginseng and an go on cooking for a while.

Directions Take it before meals, twice daily.

Indications Diarrhea.

Recipe 5

Ingredients

    chestnut   300 g
    white granulated sugar   100 g

Process Get rid of the peel of chestnut and decoct it with crystal sugar and right amount of water over a slow fire for 90 minutes, when it become paste, take it out.

Directions Take it twice or three times daily, 2 spoonful for each time.

Indications Diarrhea.

SECTION 10 Retention of Food

Recipe 1
Ingredients

    hawthorn fruit（*Fructus Crataegi*）   15 g
    germinated barley（*Fructus Hordei Germinatus*）
        10 g
    radish seed（*Semen Raphani*）   8 g
    rhubarb（*Radix et Rhizoma Rhei*）   2 g

Process   Infuse all the ingredients with boiling water.
Directions   Take it as drink, once daily.
Indications   Retention of food.

Recipe 2
Ingredients

    white radish（*Napus*）   500 – 1000 g
    honey（*Mel*）   150 – 200 g

Process   Cut the white radish into tripes or dices, heat right amount of water in an aluminum pot, when it come to boil, then add the radish and go on cooking, when it come to boil, ladle the radish out and dry it under the sun, put it in an aluminum pot and add in the honey, heat them over a slow fire with stirring, mix them well and let it cool.

Directions　Take it after meals, 30 - 50 g for each time.

Indications　Retention of food.

Recipe 3

Ingredients

　　hawthorn fruit （Fructus Crataegi·）　　　20 g
　　Chinese - date （Fructus Ziziphi Jujubae）　10
　　Chicken's gizzard - membrane （Endothelium Corneum Gigeriae Galli）　　　　　　　　　2
　　white sugar　　　　　　　　right amount

Process　Parch the slice of hawthorn fruit and Chinese - date until they are dark, then add in the membrane of the chicken's gizzard and right amount of water, go on cooking until it is well done.

Directions　Take it warmly, twice or three times daily for 2 days successively.

Indications　Retention of food.

SECTION 11 Enuresis.

Recipe 1
Ingredients

　　fragrant solomonseal rhizome (*Rhizoma Polygonati Odorati*)　　50 g

Process　Clean it up and decoct it in right amount of water.

Directions　Take it as drink.

Indications　Enuresis.

Recipe 2
Ingredients

　　bitter cardamon (*Fructus Alpiniae Oxyphyllae*)
　　　　　　　　　　　　　　　6 g

　　cherokee rose - hipe (*Fructus Rosae Laevigatae*)
　　　　　　　　　　　　　　　6 g

　　Radix Linderae　　　　　5 g

Process　Decoct all the ingredients in 3 bowls of water until half bowl of decoction left.

Directions　Take it as drink, one dose daily.

Indications Enuresis.

Recipe 3

Ingredients

    walnut kernel（*Semen Juglandis*）   100 g
    honey（*Mel*）   15 g

Process Parch the walnut kernel in a pot until it is rill, then let it dry and mix it with the honey.

Directions Take it.

Indications Enuresis.

Recipe 4

Ingredients

    dangshen（*Radix Codonopsis Pilosulae*） 15 g
    Chinese yam（*Rhizoma Dioscoreae*）   10 g
    poria（*Poria*）   10 g
    bitter cardamon（*Fructus Alpiniae Oxyphyllae*）
        8 g
    cimicifuga rhizome（*Rhizoma Cimicifugae*））
        6 g
    magnolia flower（*Flos Magnoliae*）   6 g
    prickly ash peel（*Pericarpium Citri Reticulatae*）
        3 g
    liquorice（*Radix Glycyrrhizae*）   3 g

Process Soak all the ingredients with warm water for 15 minutes, then decoct them over a slow fire for 15 minutes twice, sift out the decoction.

Directions　Take the decoction once at bedtime, one dose for two days.

Indications　Enuresis.

Recipe 5

Ingredients

　　dragon's bone (*Os Draconis Fossilia Ossis Mastodi*)　　20 g
　　Oyster shell (*Concha Ostreae*)　　290 g
　　Rhizoma Dioscoreae Bishie　　10 g
　　bitter cardamon (*Fructus Alpiniae Oxyphyllae*)　　10 g
　　Radix Linderae　　9 g
　　ginkgo nut (*Semen Ginkgo*)　　9 g
　　oriental water plantain rhizome (*Rhizoma Alismatis*)　　9 g
　　grassleaved sweetflag rhizome (*Rhizoma Acori Graminei*)　　6 g
　　liquorice (*Radix Glycyrrhizae*)　　6 g

Process　Decoct all the ingredients in 600 ml of water over a slow fire until 120 – 150 ml of decoction left.

Directions　Take it in twice or three times.

Indications　Enuresis.

SECTION 12 Rachitis

Recipe 1
Ingredients

pork bone	250 g
cuttle bone	250 g
salt	right amount

Process　Clean up the pig's bone and cuttle − bone, pound them into pieces, decoct them in right amount of water until the get a white sticky decoction, season it with the salt and condiment.

Directions　Drink the soup once or twice daily.
Indications　Rachitis.

Recipe 2
Ingredients

Siberian solomonseal rhizome (*Rhizoma Polygonati*)	100 g
honey (*Mel*)	200 g

Process　Clean up the dry Siberian solomonseal rhizome up, soak it with water until it is enlarged, heat it over a slow fire until it is well done, ladle it out and dry it. Add in the honey and mix them well, let it cool, store in a bottle for later use.

Directions　Take a spoon of it for each time.
Indications　Rachitis.

Recipe 3
Ingredients
　　luttle bone（Os Sepiellae seu Sepiae）　　10 g
　　tortoise plastron（Plastrum Testudinis）　12 g
　　rubia root（Radix Rubiae）　　　　　　　6 g
　　brown sugar　　　　　　　　　　right amount

Process　Decoct the first three ingredients in right amount of water, when it is done, add in the brown sugar.

Directions　Take it in twice or three times daily.
Indications　Rachitis.

SECTION 13 Nocturnal Fretfulness in Infants

Recipe 1
Ingredients
> wheat (*Fructus Tritici*) 15 g
> Chinese − date (*Fructus Ziziphi Jujubae*) 6 g
> liquorice (*Radix Glycyrrhizae*) 3 g
> cicada ecdysis 3 g

Process   Decoct all them in right amount of water.
Directions   Take it as drink, one dose daily.
Indications   Nocturnal fretfulness in infants.

Recipe 2
Ingredients
> polished round − grained rice (*Semen Oryzae Sativae*) 50 − 100 g
> *Cortex Cinnamomi* 3 g
> brown sugar right amount

Process   Make the rice into gruel with the water, when it is nearly done, add in the powder of bark of cinnamon in it and go on cooking until it is done, add in the brown sugar.

Pediatric Diseases

Directions   Take it warmly, once or twice daily
Indications   Nocturnal fretfulness in infants.

SECTION 14 Infantile Polysialia

Recipe 1

Ingredients

    Chinese − date（Fructus Ziziphi Jujubae）   5
    dried orange peel（Pericarpium Citri）   5 g
    lophatherum（Herba Lophatheri）   7 g

Process   Decoct all the ingredients in right amount of water.

Directions   Take it in twice, one dose daily for 3 to 5 days.

Indications   Infantile polysialia.

Recipe 2

Ingredients

    parched white atractylodes rhizome（Rhizoma Atractylodis Macrocephalae）   20 − 30 g
    bitter cardamon（Fructus Alpiniae Oxyphyllae）   20 − 30 g
    fresh ginger（Zingiberis）   50 g
    white sugar   50 g

white flour　　　　　　　　　　　　right amount

Process　Grind the parched white atractylodes rhizome into fine powder. Pound the ginger into mash to get its juice. Mix the fine powder of the flour and sugar well, make it into dough with the ginger's juice and right amount of water, then make it into 10 – 15 small cakes, toast it in a pot.

Directions　Take it twice daily, both in the morning and in the evening. one cake for each time. Take it for 7 to 10 days successively.

Indications　Infantile polysialia.

SECTION 15　Acute Nephritis in Children

Recipe 1
Ingredients
　　mulberry bark（*Cortex Mori Radicis*）　　30 g
　　white chrysanthemum flower（*Flos Chrysanthemi*）
　　　　　　　　　　　　　　　　　　　　9 g
　　mung bean（*Semen Phaseoli Radiati*）　60 g
　Process　Decoct all the ingredients in right amount of water.
　Directions　Take it in twice daily.
　Indications　Acute nephritis in children.

Recipe 2
Ingredients
　　carp　　　　　　　　　　　　1(about 500 g)
　　poria（*Poria*）　　　　　　　　　　10 g
　Process　Put the slices of poria into the cave of the carp, then decoct it with condiments such as garlic, ginger, scallion etc in right amount of water over a strong fire, when it come to boil, go on heat it over a slow fire until the carp is

well done, remove the garlic, ginger, scallion, season it with the salt.

Directions Eat the carp and drink the soup. Take it in twice daily for 7–8 days successively.

Indications Acute nephritis in children.

Recipe 3

Ingredients

    waxgourd peel (*Exocarpium Benincasae*)   20 g
    watermelon peel (*Exocarpium Citrulli*)   20 g
    white cogongrass rhizome (*Rhizoma Imperatae*)   20 g
    corn stigma (*Stigma Maydis*)   15 g
    red phaseolus bean (*Semen Phaseoli*)   200 g

Process Soak the red phaseolus bean in warm water in an earthenware pot for 1–2 hours, then add in the other ingredients and right amount of water, heat it over a strong fire, when it come to boil, go on heat it over a slow fire for half an hour, sift out the decoction from dregs.

Directions Take it warmly. Take in three times daily until the edema disappears.

Indications Acute nephritis in children.

Chapter Five
Orthopedic and Traumatic Diseases

SECTION 1 Osteomyelitis and Bone Tuberculosis

Recipe 1
Ingredients
   living shrimp   10
   crude astragalus root   15

Process   Decoct all them in right amount of water.

Directions   Take it twice daily, once in the morning and once in the evening respectively.

Indications   Bone tuberculosis, deep-rooted carbuncle of yin type, wounds hard to heal.

Recipe 2
Ingredients
   cut tobacco   100 g
   areca seed (*Semen Arecae*)   100 g

      oyster shell (*Concha Ostreae*)   50 g
      dahurian angelica root (*Radix Angelicae Dahuricae*)   50 g
      ginger juice (*Succus Zingiberis*)   right amount
      flour   right amount

Process   Grind the first four ingredients into fine powder, then make them into paste with the ginger juice and flour.

Directions   Apply it on the affected part, change it once daily.

Indications   Bone tuberculosis, septic knee.

Recipe

Ingredients

      powder of carbonized tortoise   250 g
      Chinese - date (*Fructus Ziziphi Jujubae*)   250 g

Process   Grind them into fine powder, then make them into boluses with right amount of water.

Directions   Take it once in the morning and once in the evening respectively, 12 g each time.

Indications   Osteoarticular tuberculosis.

SECTION 2 Fracture

Recipe 1
Ingredients
rosewood (*Lignum Acronychiae*)
litchi seed (*Semen Litchi*)

Process   Bake them dry and grind them into fine powder separately. Mix them well for later use.

Directions   Mix the powder with 75 per cent alcohol to make paste. Apply it on the affected part. Wrap it with disinfected gauze for 7 seven days.

Indications   Fracture. It has the effect of stop bleeding and relieving pain.

Recipe 2
Ingredients
big crab   2
spirits   right amount

Process   Bake the crab on the tile over fire, then grind it into fine powder.

Directions   Take the powder with spirits, 20 g each

time.

Indications   Fracture. It can help remove blood stasis, dredge the meridian passage and promote the healing of bone.

Recipe 3
Ingredients
   fresh crab   250 g
   millet wine   right amount

Process   Clean up the crab, then pound it into mash.

Directions   Take 150 g of the mash with hot millet wine orally, apply the surplus of the mash on the affected part.

Indications   Fracture. It can help remove blood stasis, dredge the meridian passage and promote the healing of bone.

SECTION 3 Traumata

Recipe 1
Ingredients

Chinese flowering crab apple　　　　250 g

Process   Pound the flowers into mash.

Directions   Apply the mash on the affected area, change the dressing once every 12 hours.

Indications   Traumata with severe swelling pain. It can cool the blood and has the effect of detumescence.

Recipe 2
Ingredients

Chinese yeast　　　　　　　right amount
fresh rehmannia root（*Radix Rehmanniae*）
　　　　　　　　　　　　　right amount

Process   Pound them into mash, then stew it hot.

Directions   Apply the hot mash on the affected part, change it once daily.

Indications   Acute stremma or contusion.

Recipe 3

Ingredients

fresh scallion stalks (*Bulbus Allii Fistulosi*)	60 g
prickly ash peel (*Pericarpium Zanthozxyli*)	12 g
borneol (*Borneolum*)	0.6 g

Process Clean up the stalk of the scallion, pound it into mash. Grind the prickly ash peel and borneol into fine powder, mix them with the mash to make a paste.

Directions Apply it on the affected part. Change the dressing once daily.

Indications Sprain of ankle with swelling pain and limitation of movement.

Recipe 4

Ingredients

root of rose (*Radix Rosae Rugosae*)	25 g
millet wine	right amount

Process Clean the root of the rose up and decoct it in the millet wine.

Directions Take it in twice, both in the morning and in the evening. It can promote the circulation of both qi and blood to relieve pain.

Indications Traumata.

Chapter Six Dermatoses

SECTION 1 Urticaria

Urticaria, or hives, is an allergic disease caused by contact with a specific precipitating factor (allergen). Some food, drugs, parasites, etc. can act as the allergens. It is marked by raised edematous patches of skin and mucous membrane and usually by intense itching. It is called "fēng zhěn kuài" in traditional Chinese medicine.

Recipe 1
Ingredients
    black plum (*Fructus Nume*)　　　　　9 g
    ledebouriella root (*Radix Ledebouriellae*)
    　　　　　　　　　　　　　　　　　9 g
    bupleurum root (*Radix Bupleuri*)　　　9 g
    schisandra fruit (*Fructus Schisandrae*)　6 g
    liquorice (*Radix Glycyrrhizae*)　　　　10 g

Process Decoct all the ingredients in right amount of water.

Directions Take the decoction orally, twice daily.

Indications Hives due to retention of wind – heat evil and dampness due to dysfunction of spleen, marked by wheals, intense itching, aversion to cold and mild fever, pantalgia, etc..

Recipe 2

Ingredients

    white batryticated silkworm (*Bombyx Batryticatus*)   10 g

    schizonpeta spike (*Spica Schizonepeta*)   10 g

    cicada slough (*Periostracum Cicadae*)   5 g

Process Decoct them in right amount of water.

Directions Take it twice daily.

Indications Hives, cutaneous pruritus.

Recipe 3

Ingredients

    dried litchi (*Fructus litchi*)   14

    brown sugar   30 g

Process Remove the stone and peel of the litchi, decoct it in right amount of water, season it with brown sugar.

Directions Take it one dose daily for 2 weeks successively.

Indications　Hives with recurrent wheals.

Recipe 4

Ingredients

　　waxgourd peel (*Exocarpium Benincasae*)

　　　　　　　　　　　　　　　　20 g

　　chrysanthemum flower (*Flos Chrysanthemi*)

　　　　　　　　　　　　　　　　15 g

　　red peony root (*Radix Paeoniae Rubra*)　12 g

　　honey (*Mel*)　　　　　　　right amount

Process　Decoct the first three ingredients in water, sift out the decoction from dregs. Season the decoction with honey. Mix the decoction and honey well for later use.

Directions　Take it as drink, one dose daily for a week successively.

Indications　Hives with red wheals.

SECTION 2 Neurodermatitis

Recipe 1
Ingredients
>   old tea leaves (*Thea*)   6 g
>   *argyi leaf* (*Folium Artemisiae Argyi*)   6 g
>   *ginger* (*Zingiberis*)   50 g
>   *purple - skin garlic* (*Bulbus Allii*)   2
>   *table salt*   right amount

Process Decoct the first four ingredients in right amount of water, season the decoction with salt.

Directions Wash the affected part with the decoction. One dose every two days.

Indications Neurodermatitis. It can alleviate the symptoms in some degree.

Recipe 2
Ingredients
>   *fresh olives*   1000 g

Process Wash the olives clean and remove the stones. Pound them into mash, decoct it in 1000 g water over a slow fire, until the decoction becomes green, then let it stand for half an hour, sift out the decoction.

Directions   Spread it on the affected part or wash the affected part with the decoction several times daily.

Indications   Dermatitis.

Recipe 3
Ingredients
   tea leaves (*Thea*)   60 g
   alum (*Alumen*)   60 g

Process   Soak them in water for half an hour, then decoct them for half an hour.

Directions   Soak the hand and feet in the warm decoction for 10 minutes, then let them dry naturally.

Indications   Dermatitis due to long – term work in water, marked by intense itching, erythema, and blisters.

Recipe 4
Ingredients
   greenbrier (*Rhizoma Smilacis Glabrae*)   30 g
   flesh of pangolin (*Manis Pentadactyla*)   60 g
   condiments   right amount

Process   Clean greenbrier up and wrap it with gauze, decoct it with the pangolin in right amount of water, when it is done, season it with salt and other condiments.

Dermatoses

Directions　Eat the meat and drink the soup. Take it twice daily for 10 days successively.

Indications　Dermatitis with severe pain, especially at nights, or xerosis cutis.

SECTION 3 Eczema

Eczema, or weeping dermatitis, is an inflammatory condition of the skin characterized by redness, itching, and oozing vesicular lesions, which become scaly, crusted, or hardened. It often affects the face, retroauricular part, back of the hand, breasts, scrotum, fossa cubitalis, popliteal regions and legs, etc.. The redness, lesions, blisters are symmetric respectively. The affected regions reveal severe itching, burning pains. The disease is recurrent.

Recipe 1
Ingredients
 black - snake　　　　　　　　　　　　15 g
 Chinese angelica root（*Radix Angelicae Sinensis*）
　　　　　　　　　　　　　　　　　　　9 g
 fragrant solomonseal rhizome（*Rhizoma Polygonati Odorati*）　　　　　　　　　　5 g
 Process　Decoct them in right amount of water.
 Directions　Take it in twice daily for 10 days successively.

Indications　Eczema with intense itching, xerosis, lesions and pachyderma.

Recipe 2

Ingredients

lotus	5
polished glutinous rice (*Semen Oryzae Glutinosae*)	100 g
crystal sugar	15 g

Process　Make the rice into gruel with water, when it is nearly done, add in the crystal sugar and lotus flower and go on cooking for a while.

Directions　take it as breakfast. Once daily. One week successively consisted of one course.

Indications　Eczema with rashes, blisters, lesions, intense itching or alternate itching and pain.

Recipe 3

Ingredients

Flour of green gram (*Semen Phaseoli Radiati*)

	30 g
honey (*Mel*)	9 g
borneol (*Borneolum*)	3 g
vinegar	30 g

Process　Stir-fry the powder of green grams until it becomes gray, then mix it with honey and borneol and vinegar to make gruel. Spread it on a piece of oilpaper in the center of which an eyelet is made.

Directions   Apply the oilpaper on the affected part, once every two days.

Indications   Weeping dermatitis.

Recipe 4

Ingredients

white sugar   120 g

Process   Pour 2000 g of water in an aluminium pot, add in the sugar, when it comes to boil, then pour the liquid into a basin.

Directions   Fumigate and wash the affected part with hot decoction twice daily for 2 days.

Indications   Eczema of the scrotum.

Dermatoses

SECTION 4 Herpes Zoster

Herpes zoster, or shingles, is an acute viral inflammation of the sensory ganglia of spinal and cranial nerves associated with a vesicular eruption and neuralgic pain and caused by reactivation of the herpesvirus causing chicken pox. The course lasts 3 – 5 days. Recurrence is seldom seen after recovering.

Recipe 1
Ingredients
　fresh portulaca (*Herba Portulacae*)
Process　Clean it up and cut it into small sections, then pound them into mash.
Directions　Apply it on the affected part twice daily.
Indications　Shingles. It can clear away heat evil to remove blood stasis and relieve swelling.

Recipe 2
Ingredients
　snake slough (*Pillis Ophidiae*)　　right amount

Chapter Six

    sesame oil   right amount

Process   Stir－fry the snake slough over a slow fire with its nature retained. Then grind it into powder, add in sesame oil to make gruel.

Directions   Apply the gruel on the affected part, twice or three times daily.

Indications   Shingles.

Recipe 3

Ingredients

    alum（*Alumen*）   10 g
    amber   3 g
    borneol（*Borneolum*）   4 g
    centipede（*Scolopendra*）（*Baked and ground into fine powder*）   2

Process   Grind all the ingredients into fine powder, then make the powder into paste with the egg white.

Directions   Spread the paste on the affected part several times daily.

Indications   Herpes zoster.

Recipe 4

Ingredients

    root of fresh Chinese chives（*Radix Allii Tuberosi*）
                                                  30 g
    fresh earthworm（*Lumbricus*）   20 g

Dermatoses

  sesame oil   right amount

 Process Pound the first two ingredients into mash, then mix them with a small amount of sesame oil well.

 Directions Spread it on affected part twice daily.

 Indications Shingles.

Recipe 5

Ingredients

realgar	1 g
catechu (*Nauclea Gambir*)	1 g
white alum	1 g
borneol (*Borneolum*)	0.5 g
Vaseline	5 g

 Process Grind all them into fine powder, then mix the powder with 5 g of Vaseline to make ointment.

 Directions Spread the ointment on the affected part, twice or three times daily.

 Indications Herpes zoster.

SECTION 5 Acne

Acne is a disorder of the skin caused by inflammation of the skin glands and hair follicles. The disease is commonly seen during adolescence, more male cases than females. It often affects the face, upper chest and back.

Recipe 1
Ingredients
  red sage root (*Radix Salviae Miltiorrhizae*)
                                                           100 g
Process Grind it into fine powder, then store it in a bottle for later use.
Directions Take it three times daily, 3 g for each time.
Indications Acne.

Recipe 2
Ingredients
  loquat leaf (*Folium Eriobotryae*)
  prunella spike (*Spica Prunellae*)
  mulberry bark (*Cortex Mori Radicis*)

Dermatoses

    honeysuckle flower（Flos Lonicerae）
    forsythia fruit（Fructus Forsythiae）
    scutellaria root（Radix Scutellariae）
    bryozoatum
    liquorice（Radix Glycyrrhizae）

Process   Decoct all the ingredients twice in water, sift out the decoctions and mix them well.

Directions   Take it in twice, one dose daily.

Indications   Acne.

Recipe 3

Ingredients

red sage root（Radix Salviae Miltiorrhizae）	15 g
scutellaria root（Radix Scutellariae）	12 g
raw capejasmine fruit（Fructus Gardeniae）	12 g
mulberry bark（Cortex Mori Radicis）	12 g
Moutan bark（Cortex Moutan Radicis）	12 g
red peony root（Radix Paeoniae Rubra）	12 g
forsythia fruit（Fructus Forsythiae）	9 g
rhubarb（Radix et Rhizoma Rhei）	3 g
raw liquorice（Radix Glycyrrhizae）	3 g

Process   Decoct them in right amount of water twice, sift out the decoctions and mix them well.

Directions   Take it in twice daily, one dose daily.

Indications　Acne.

Recipe 4
Ingredients
　　raw hawthorn fruit (*Fructus Crataegi*)　30 g
　　reed Rhizome (*Rhizoma Phragmitis*)　30 g
　　crystal sugar　　　　　　　　right amount
Process　Decoct them in right amount of water.
Directions　Take the decoction as drink, twice daily.
Indications　Acne.

SECTION 6　Miliaria (Prickly Heat)

Miliaria is an inflammatory disorder of the skin characterized by redness, eruption, burning or itching, and the release of sweat in abnormal ways (as by the eruption of vesicles) due to blockage of the ducts of the sweat glands. The disease mentioned here refers to especially prickly heat, a noncontagious cutaneous eruption of red pimples with intense itching and tingling. It is commonly seen in summer. It is easy to affect infants, cases of fat build, and chronic patients.

Recipe 1
Ingredients
 waxgourd (*Fructus Benincasae*)　　200 – 400 g
 coix seed (*Semen Coicis*)　　　　　30 – 50 g
 salt　　　　　　　　　　　　right amount

Process　Cut the waxgourd into cubes, then decoct it with coix seed in right amount of water to make gruel, season it with salt.

Directions　Eat the waxgourd and drink the gruel.

Take it several times a day, one dose every other day. 3 to 5 successive doses consisted of one course.

Indications   Prickly heat.

Recipe 2

Ingredients

Flour of green gram (*Semen Phaseoli Radiati*)
talc powder (*Pulvis Talcum*)

Process   Take the two ingredients in equal portion, then mix them well.

Directions   Wash the affected part, then apply the mixture on the affected part.

Indications   Prickly heat.

Recipe 3

Ingredients

fresh luffa leaf (*Folium Luffae*)

Process   Clean it up and cut it into piece, then pound them into mash, extract its juice with a gauze cloth.

Directions   Spread it on the affected part once or twice daily.

Indications   Heat rashes.

Dermatoses

SECTION 7　Chilblain

Chilblain is an inflammatory swelling or sore caused by exposure (as of the hands or feet) to cold. Coldness and dampness may cause local poor blood circulation, leading to tissue ischemia and consequent cellular injuries. The swellings have no obvious borders, often accompanied with itching or numbness, burning, etc.. It is commonly seen in winter recurrently.

Recipe 1
Ingredients
 cinnamon twig (*Ramulus Cinnamomi*) 30 g
 Capsicum (*Fructus Capsici*) 30 g
 rehmannia root (*Radix Rehmanniae*) 30 g
 safflower (*Flos Carthami*) 10 g

Process Decoct all the ingredients in right amount of water to get 4 liters of decoction.

Directions Fumigate and wash the affected part with the decoction once or twice daily.

Indications Perniones.

Recipe 2

Ingredients

Chinese angelica root (*Radix Angelicae Sinensis*)	50 g
safflower (*Flos Carthami*)	50 g
vaccaria seed (*Semen Vaccariae*)	50 g
dried ginger (*Rhizoma Zingiberis*)	30 g
cinnamon twig (*Ramulus Cinnamomi*)	30 g
capsicum (*Fructus Capsici*)	30 g
asarum herb (*Herba Asari*)	10 g
camphor	10 g
borneol (*Borneolum*)	10 g
alcohol (75%)	750 ml

Process Soak all the ingredients in alcohol for a week. Then get the tincture with a gauze and store it in a bottle for later use.

Directions Spread it on the affected part with cotton for three to five times daily.

Indications Perniones.

Recipe 3

Ingredients

cassia bark (*Cortex Cinnamomi*)	30 g
red capsicum (*Fructus Capsici*)	15 g
camphor	9 g

Dermatoses

borneol (*Borneolum*)	3 g
spirits	250 ml

Process Soak the first two ingredients in right amount of water for 5 days, sift out the tincture from dregs, then grind the borneol and camphor into fine powder, and add them in the tincture.

Directions Spread the tincture on the affected part three to five times daily.

Indications Perniones.

Chapter Seven
Diseases of Eyes, Ears, Nose, and Throat

SECTION 1 Acute Conjunctivitis

Acute conjunctivitis refers to acute inflammation of the conjunctiva. It is called "tianxing chiyan", "baofa huoyan" in traditional Chinese medicine.

Recipe 1
Ingredients
    coptis（*Rhizoma Coptidis*）   30 g
    trichosanthes root（*Radix Trichosanthis*）
        30 g
    chrysanthemum flower（*Flos Chrysanthemi*）
        30 g
    Chuanxiong Rhizome （*Rhizoma Ligustici Chuanxiong*）   30 g
    mint（*Herba Menthae*）   30 g

forsythia fruit (*Fructus Forsythiae*)　　30 g
　　　phellodendron bark (*Cortex Phellodendri*)
　　　　　　　　　　　　　　　　　　　　180 g
　　　tea leaves (*Thea*)　　　　　　　　360 g

Process　Grind all them into raw powder, then mix them well.

Directions　Infuse the powder with boiling water for 10 minutes. Take it three times daily, 6 g each time.

Indications　Acute conjunctivitis accompanied with constipation.

Recipe 2
Ingredients
　　　chrysanthemum flower (*Flos Chrysanthemi*)
　　　　　　　　　　　　　　　　　　　　10 g
　　　tea　　　　　　　　　　　　　　　3 g

Process　Infuse them with boiling water for 5 – 10 minutes.

Directions　Take it as drink, one dose daily.

Indications　Conjunctivitis due to hyperactivity of liver – fire.

Recipe 3
Ingredients
　　　white Juda's ear　　　　　　　　　30 g
　　　tea　　　　　　　　　　　　　　　6 g

crystal sugar   50 g

Process   Decoct them in right amount of water.

Directions   Take it one dose daily for several days successively.

Indications   Conjunctivitis.

Recipe 4

Ingredients

dandelion herb (*Herba Taraxaci*)   60 g

Process   Decoct it in right amount of water.

Directions   Take it twice daily for several days.

Indications   Conjunctivitis

SECTION 2 Ulcerative Blepharitis

Ulcerative blepharitis refers to inflammation esp. of the margins of the eyelids with ulceration.

Recipe 1
Ingredients
    gentian root（*Radix Gentianae*）   9 g
    tea leaves（*Thea*）   9 g
    white alum   3 g
    halite（*Halitum*）   3 g
    safflower（*Flos Carthami*）   3 g
    liquorice（*Radix Glycyrrhizae*）   3 g
    ledebouriella root（*Radix Ledebouriellae*）
        6 g
    mulberry leaf（*Folium Mori*）   6 g
    fresh apricot kernel（*Semen Armeniacae*）
        7
    chrysanthemum flower（*Flos Chrysanthe-*

mi）　　　　　　　　　　　　　　　10 g

Process　Decoct all them in right amount of water, sift out the decoction.

Directions　Wash eyes with the decoction.

Indications　Ulcerative blepharitis.

Recipe 2

Ingredients

　　atractylodes rhizome（*Rhizoma Atractylodis*）　　　　　　　　　　　　　　10 g

　　dahurian Angelica root（*Radix Angelicae Dahuricae*）　　　　　　　　　　6 g

　　peppermint（*Herba Menthae*）　6 g

　　honeysuckle flower（*Flos Lonicerae*）　　　　　　　　　　　　　　　　6 g

Process　Decoct them in 200 ml of water until it come to boil.

Directions　Fumigate the affected eye with the decoction for 10 – 20 minutes, three to five times daily.

Indications　Ulcerative blepharitis.

Dermatoses

SECTION 3 Nyctalopia

Nyctalopia, or night blindness, refers to reduced visual capacity in faint light, as at night.

Recipe 1
Ingredients

mutton liver	500 g
starch	right amount
soya sauce	right amount
vinegar	right amount

Process   Cut the goat liver into slices, then mix them with wet starch, stir — fry it over a strong fire for a while, then add in soya sauce and vinegar and stew for a while.

Directions   Take the slices of mutton liver along with other foods for several days.

Indications   Night blindness.

Recipe 2
Ingredients

prepared abalone shell (*Concha Haliotidis Praeparata*)　　　　　　　　　　30 g
polished round－grained rice (*Semen Oryzae Sativae*)　　　　　　　　　　100 g

Process　Pound the calcined abalone shell into pieces, then heat it with 200 ml of water over a strong fire for an hour, then sift out the decoction from dregs, then add in 600 ml of water and rice, go on cooking to make thin gruel.

Directions　Take the gruel once daily.

Indications　Night blindness.

Recipe 3

Ingredients

sweet potato leaves　　　　　　150－200 g
mutton liver　　　　　　　　　　200 g

Process　Clean up the sweet potato leaves and cut them into pieces, cut the goat liver into slices, then decoct all the ingredients in right amount of water.

Directions　Eat the liver and drink the soup, once daily for three days.

Indications　Night blindness.

SECTION 4 Glaucoma

Recipe
Ingredients

turnip seed	right amount
spirits	right amount
honey (*Mel*)	right amount

Process Soak turnip seeds in spirits over night, then steam them over boiled water for 20 minutes, dry them and grind them into fine powder. Mix the powder with honey to make it into small pills as large as mung bean.

Directions Take it with gruel of rice twice daily, 10 g each time.

Indications Glaucoma.

SECTION 5 Chronic Rhinitis

Chronic rhinitis is a chronic inflammatory change o the nasal mucosa, mainly due to the protraction of acute rhinitis. Its main symptom is nasal obstruction. This disease is called "Bí zhì" (nasal obstruction) in traditional Chinese medicine.

ETIOLOGY AND PATHOGENESIS

It is related to *qi* deficiency of the lung and spleen which fails o protect the body from being attacked by pathogenic factors, and which leaves the evils and toxins to linger in the body, resulting in accumulation of the evils in meridians and collaterals, stagnation of *qi* and *blood* as well as nasal obstruction.

MAIN SYMPTOMS AND SIGNS

1. Intermittent, alternative or continuous nasal obstruction.

2. Swelling or hypertrophy of nasal mucosa, which is as big as mulberry fruit and in dark − red color, especially in inferior nasal concha.

MAIN POINTS OF DIAGNOSIS

1. The nasal obstruction is either alternate, intermittent or continuous.
2. The nasal mucosa swells or becomes thick, especially that of the inferior nasal concha.
3. Hyposmia is fluctuating.
4. There is pain and itching in the throat and tinnitus or hypoacusis may occur.

Recipe 1
Ingredients
    magnolia flower (*Flos Magnoliae*)   30 g
    egg   10

Process   Decoct them right amount of water until the eggs are well done.

Directions   Eat the eggs and drink the soup. Take them twice daily, one dose every five days and two or three doses successively are needed.

Indications   Chronic rhinitis.

Recipe 2

Ingredients

> *mulberry leaf* (*Folium Mori*)   9 g
> *sweet apricot kernel* (*Semen Armeniacae Dulce*)   9 g
> *chrysanthemum flower* (*Flos Chrysanthemi*)   6 g
> *polished round – grained rice* (*Semen Oryzae Sativae*)   60 g

Process   Decoct the mulberry and chrysanthemum in right amount of water for 15 minutes, sift out the decoction from dregs, then add in the sweat apricot and rice and go on cooking to make a gruel.

Directions   Take it once daily for several days.

Indications   Chronic rhinitis.

Recipe 3

Ingredients

> *astragalus root* (*Radix astragali seu Hedysari*)   10 g
> *rehmannia root* (*Radix Rehmanniae*)   10 g
> *black plum* (*Fructus Nume*)   10 g
> *Herba Siegesbeckia Orientalis*   10 g
> *ledebouriella root* (*Radix Ledebouriellae*)   6 g
> *bupleurum root* (*Radix Bupleuri*)   3 g
> *honey* (*Mel*)   30 g

Dermatoses

Process   Decoct all them in right amount of water.
Directions   Take in twice daily.
Indications   Chronic rhinitis.

SECTION 6 Acute and Chronic Nasosinusitis

Acute nasosinusitis is an acute nonspecific inflammation of the mucous membrane of the frontal sinus, ethmoid sinus and maxillary sinus (sphenoiditis is seldom seen). Its clinical characteristics are fever, headache, nasal obstruction and purulent nasal discharge. It belongs to the category of "Bí yuān" (rhinorrhea with turbid discharge) in traditional Chinese medicine.

ETIOLOGY AND PATHOGENESIS

It is related to the pathogenic factors which invade and attack the human body and mix with the heat in the lung, spleen and gallbladder, ascending to the orifice of the nose, steaming and burning the muscular membrane of the nasal sinuses.

MAIN SYMPTOMS AND SIGNS

1. Decrease of smelling ability in the attack of nasal ob-

struction.

2. Profuse and purulent nasal discharge at the initial time yellow and white thick nasal discharge, and then yellow, turbid and tenacious nasal discharge with stinking odor and difficulty to blow of.

3. Splitting headache or distention and discomfort in the head. headache varies with the condition of sick sinuses, mostly appearing in the superficial skull in sinusitis of the anterior group of sinuses or in deep location in sinusitis of posterior group of sinuses.

4. There is painful sensation from percussion on the surface of projection of sinuses. There are obvious congestion and swelling in the nasal mucosa, especially severe redness and swelling in the middle nasal concha; there is a large volume of tenacious purulent secretion can be seen in meatus concha ethmoturbinalis majoris and rhinal fissure after nasal discharge is blown out.

MAIN POINTS OF DIAGNOSIS

1. Mostly the patient has a history of upper respiratory tract infection or of being choked in water when swimming.

2. The patient has headache or pain in the area of nasal sinuses which may be distending, stabbing or jumping and may occur at a specific time (for instance in the case of maxillary sinusitis or frontal sinusitis, mild in the morning, se-

vere at noon and gradually relieved again in the afternoon).
Examination will find tenderness in the corresponding areas
of the nasal sinuses.

3. The nasal obstruction is alternate or intermittent, and accompanied with hyposmia.

4. There is much sticky or yellow purulent nasal discharge.

5. The nasal mucosa swells, with purulent secretion flowing out from or accumulating in the nasal meatus to which the relevant sinuses open.

X－ray photograph shows that the corresponding nasal sinuses are of low degree of transparency and there is cloudiness or fluid level (take maxillary sinusitis for instance).

7. There are general symptoms such as aversion to cold, running fever and being uncomfortable all over.

Chronic nasosinusitis, mostly caused by unthorough－going treatment of acute nasosinusitis or by its repeated occurrences, often attacks several nasal sinuses simultaneously. Its clinical features are pus－like nasal discharge and nasal obstruction. It also falls into the category of "Bí yuān" which refers to rhinorrhea with turbid discharge.

ETIOLOGY AND PATHOGENESIS

It is related to deficiency of the lung and spleen which fail to protect the surface and fail to expel pathogenic evils, resulting in rough flow of qi and blood in the nose, and dysfunction in fluid transportation and transformation, which in turn causes accumulation of pathogenic damp and turbidity in the nose, and hence decay as well as suppuration.

MAIN SYMPTOMS AND SIGNS

1. A large volume of lingering, tenacious and white nasal discharge without stinking odor, decrease of smelling ability, intermittent severity of nasal obstruction, nasal obstruction relieved after blowing the nose and aggravated by exposure to wind and cold.

2. Slight red swelling in nasal mucosa, purulent secretion in meatus concha ethmoturbinalis majoris and rhinal fissure.

3. Pale tongue, thin and white tongue coating, soft and slow and feeble pulse.

4. Accompanied by dizziness, distending sensation in the head, bradyphrenia, shortness of breath, lassitude, low voice, reluctance in speaking.

MAIN POINTS OF DIAGNOSIS

1. Much sticky and white or thick and yellow pus – like nasal discharge flows out from the nose, often blown out through the anterior narises or inhaled in through the posteri-

or narises and then spit out.

2. Nasal obstruction is alternate or intermittent, and may be relieved after the nasal discharge is blown out. If polyp is formed the obstruction will be continuous.

3. Osphresis is obtuse.

4. The inferior nasal concha is swollen, with pus-like discharge in the middle nasal meatus and the olfactory cleft. The middle nasal concha may show hypertrophy or polypoid change and polyp may be formed in the middle nasal meatus.

5. **X-ray** photo of the nasal sinuses often shows that the shadows of the cavities of the nasal sinuses have darkened and the mucous membranes thickened, or sign of empyema in the cavities of the sinuses may be present.

6. The patient has a feeling of heaviness, fullness, distending pain and discomfort in the head.

Recipe 1

Ingredients

astragalus root (*Radix astragali seu Hedysari*)
15 g

tangerine peel (*Pericarpium Citri Reticulatae*)
15 g

lotus leaf (*Folium Nelumbinis*) 1

Process   Decoct the first two ingredients in right amount of water, sift out the decoction from dregs, then soak the lotus leaf in the decoction for 20 minutes, sift out

Dermatoses

the decoction.

    Directions   Take it as drink once daily for 15 days.
    Indications   Nasosinusitis.

Recipe 2

Ingredients

fresh luffa stem (*Luffae*)	30 g
mulberry leaf (*Folium Mori*)	30 g

Process   Decoct all them in right amount of water.
Directions   Take it as drink once daily for a week.
Indications   Nasosinusitis.

Recipe 3

Ingredients

reed Rhizome (*Rhizoma Phragmitis*)	30 g
honeysuckle flower (*Flos Lonicerae*)	20 g
dangshen (*Radix Codonopsis Pilosulae*)	20 g
scutellaria root (*Radix Scutellariae*)	15 g
coix seed (*Semen Coicis*)	15 g
liquorice (*Radix Glycyrrhizae*)	6 g

Process   Decoct them in water.
Directions   Take it in twice, one dose daily.
Indications   Nasosinusitis.

Recipe 4

Ingredients

magnolia flower (*Flos Magnoliae*)	15 g
Fructus Xanthii	15 g
dahurian Angelica root (*Radix Angelicae Dahuricae*)	10 g
asarum herb (*Herba Asari*)	5 g
peppermint (*Herba Menthae*)	3 g
borneol (*Borneolum*)	1 g

Process Grind the first five ingredients into fine powder, mix the powder with borneol well, store it in a bottle for later use.

Directions Wrap 0.3 – 0.5 g of the mixture with cotton and put it in the nose, once or twice daily.

Indications Nasosinusitis.

SECTION 7 Epistaxis

Epistaxis (rhinorrhagia) is a common clinical symptom caused by many reasons and happening in various diseases. In mild cases, only nasal discharge is mixed with blood, and in severe cases it may endanger the patient's life.

ETIOLOGY AND PATHOGENESIS

The most common sites of nasal bleeding are the mucosal vessels over the cartilaginous nasal septum and the anterior tip of the inferior turbinate. Bleeding is usually due to external trauma, nose picking, nasal infection, or drying of the nasal site cannot be seen; these can cause great problems in management. If the blood drains into the pharynx and is swallowed, nosebleed may escape diagnosis. In these cases, bloody vomitus may be the first clue.

Underlying causes of nosebleed such as blood dyscrasia, hypertension, hemorrhagic disease, nasal tumors, and certain infectious diseases (measles or rheumatic fever) must be considered in any case of recurrent or profuse nosebleed without obvious causes.

In traditional Chinese medicine, the condition is termed "Bí nǜ", which simply means epistaxis, "Bí hóng" (flood-like nosebleed), "Hóng hàn" (red sweat) and is thought to be caused by dry lungs.

ETIOLOGY AND PATHOGENESIS

The reasons of rhinorrhagia can be listed in the following:

1. **Heat Preponderance**: It indicates hat the invaded pathogenic heat mixes with internal accumulated heat and causes hyperactivity o heat in the lung and stomach, resulting in crazy circulation of blood;

2. **Reverse-flowing** qi: For example, frustration and anger turn the stagnation of liver qi into fire which flares and brings blood upwards, pushing blood to circulate outside of vessels;

3. **Yin Deficiency in the Lung and Kidney**: It refers to flaming-up of deficient fire which injures collaterals in the nose;

4. **Spleen Qi Deficiency**: It refers to dysfunction of spleen qi which fails to restrain *blood* to circulate inside the blood vessels, causing extravasation. Also there is nasal bleeding due to trauma, which is regarded as syndrome of blood stasis.

MAIN SYMPTOMS AND SIGNS

1. In mild case, there is bloody nasal discharge or slight nasal bleeding. In severe cases, there is gushing nasal bleeding, very often at sudden onset. The blood can flow out from the anterior nostrils and also can flow into the throat via posterior nasal nostrils. The nasal bleeding can be intermittent, recurrent and continuous and can happen in one nostril and also can happen in both nostrils.

2. There is capillarectasia or bleeding spots in the anterior part of nasal septum. In severe nasal bleeding, it is not easy to notice bleeding location, and only possible to see gushing bleeding location after cleaning away the blood in the nose. Extensive blood oozing in nasal mucosa can be noticed in recurrent cases.

MAIN POINTS OF DIAGNOSIS

1. Try to find the spot of nosebleed. Bleeding is apt to occur in the mucous membrane of Kiesselbach's area.

2. Try to analyze the causes of nosebleed. Detailed inquiry about the history of the case should be made. If possible, examinations of the nasal cavity and nasopharynx, blood text, blood pressure determination, fundus examination and other necessary checks should be done.

3. The condition depends on the location and the quantity of the nosebleed. Shock may occur in severe cases. Repeated occurrence can cause anemia.

Recipe 1
Ingredients
    mulberry leaf (*Folium Mori*)   9 g
    chrysanthemum flower (*Flos Chrysanthemi*)
                                            6 g
    white cogongrass rhizome (*Rhizoma Imperatae*)
                                           15 g
    white sugar   right amount
Process   Decoct all the ingredients in right amount of water, sift out the decoction from dregs.
Directions   Take it one dose daily for several days.
Indications   Nosebleed.

Recipe 2
Ingredients
    peanut kernel with red skin (*Semen Arachidis*)
                                           15 g
    jujube (*Fructus Ziziphi Jujubae*)   15 g
Process   Decoct them in right amount of water.
Directions   Take it one dose daily, one course consists of 7 days.
Indications   Nosebleed.

Recipe 3

Ingredients

fresh shepherd's purse (*Herba Capsellae*) 90 g

Chinese-date (*Fructus Ziziphi Jujubae*) 5

Process   Decoct all them in right amount of water, sift out the decoction from dregs.

Directions   Eat the Chinese-dates and drink the soup.

Indications   Nosebleed.

Chapter Six

SECTION 8　Acute Suppurative Otitis Media

Acute suppurative otitis media refers to acute infection caused by invasion of suppurative bacteria in mucous membrane and periost of the middle ear. Clinically it is characterized by ear pain, fever, and ps effusion in the ear. It is similar to the category of "shí zhèng nóng ěr" (suppurative ear of excessive type) in traditional Chinese medicine. It is a commonly seen in otology and often happens in children.

ETIOLOGY AND PATHOGENESIS

It is due to invasion of pathogenic wind and heat evils which go to the ear through meridians, and causes accumulation of heat − toxin, and hence the accumulated heat steams and burns tympanic membrane, resulting in decay of blood and flesh and in turn perforation of tympanic membrane; or it is due to the affection of exogenous pathogenic factors, emotional factors and fire created from stagnation of liver *qi* which are sent upward to the ear orifice along the *Gall-*

bladder Meridian, resulting in the mixture of the external and internal evils, and hence causing suppuration and perforation in tympanic membrane.

MAIN SYMPTOMS AND SIGNS

1. Ear pain, even throbbing pain, is progressively aggravated so that sleeping often would be influenced. As soon as tympanic membrane perforates or is incised, ear pain and body temperature would be relieved and decreased markedly.

2. Accompanied by high fever, aversion to cold, headache and uncomfortable sensation in the whole body.

3. Conductive decrease of hearing ability, accompanied by tinnitus.

4. Local or diffuse congestion in tympanic membrane, or external prominence of tympanic membrane can be noticed. At the initial stage, perforating in pars tensa of tympanic membrane is small, with flashing and throbbing pus effusion which is in bloody fluid at the beginning and in purulence at the later stage, hence perforation enlarges.

MAIN POINTS OF DIAGNOSIS

1. This disease is in most cases caused by upper respiratory tract infection or the dirty water which gets into the

ear, most often seen at the end of winter and the beginning of spring as well as in summer. Infants are especially vulnerable to this disease.

2. There is pain in the ear. In severe cases, a throbbing pain my be present. After pus is discharged from the ear, the pain is relieved.

3. Pus comes out from the ear, at first white in color or with a little blood in it, and then yellow, thick and profuse pus runs out.

4. At the early stage the drum membrane is marked by diffuse hyperemia, looking bright red or dull red and bulging. Then perforation of tympanic membrane appears with pus running out. If the pus cannot get out easily, a pulsating discharge may be seen. If the hole is big, the pus will gush out.

5. The tinnitus is of low pitch and the deafness sound — conductive.

6. The patient may have a fever, headache and stuffy and running nose. Infant cases or patients of children may keep crying and be unquiet. The infantile patients may refuse to suck.

Recipe 1
Ingredients
red sage root (*Radix Salviae Miltiorrhizae*)
5 g

    Chuanxiong Rhizome (*Rhizoma Ligustici Chuanxiong*)   5 g
    tea leaves (*Thea*)   3 g

Process   Infuse all the ingredients with boiling water.

Directions   Take it as drink.

Indications   Acute suppurative otitis media.

Recipe 2

Ingredients

    wolfberry fruit (*Fructus Lycii*)   10 g
    Siberian solomonseal rhizome (*Rhizoma Polygonati*)   10 g
    crystal sugar   10 g

Process   Grind the Siberian solomonseal rhizome into raw powder, then infuse it with wolfberry fruit and crystal sugar with boiling water.

Directions   Take it as drink one dose daily for 15 days.

Indications   Acute suppurative otitis media.

Recipe 3

Ingredients

    honeysuckle flower (*Flos Lonicerae*)   10 g
    scutellaria root (*Radix Scutellariae*)   6 g
    white sugar   30 g

Process   Decoct the honeysuckle flower and scutellaria root in right amount of water, when it is done, season it with sugar.

　　Directions　Take it warmly twice daily for 10 days.
　　Indications　Acute suppurative otitis media.

Recipe 4
Ingredients
　　Semen Dolichoris　　　　　　　　　　20 g
　　Chinese yam (*Rhizoma Dioscoreae*)　　18 g
　　white atractylodes rhizome (*Rhizoma Atractylodis Macrocephalae*)　　15 g
　　coix seed (*Semen Coicis*)　　　　　　20 g
　　round - polished glutinous rice (*Semen Oryzae Sativae*)　　50 g

Process　Decoct white atractylodes rhizome in right amount of water, remove the dregs, then add in other ingredients and go on cooking.

　　Directions　Take it one dose daily.
　　Indications　Acute suppurative otitis media.

Recipe 5
Ingredients
　　black carp gallbladder　　　　　　　　10 g
　　alum (*Alumen*)　　　　　　　　　　　10 g
　　coptis root (*Rhizoma Coptidis*)　　　　5 g
　　borneol (*Borneolum*)　　　　　　　　0.3 g

Process　Grind all the ingredients into fine powder for

Dermatoses

later use.

Directions　Blow small amount of the powder into middle ear.

Indications　Suppurative otitis media.

Chapter Six

SECTION 9 Acute and Chronic Pharyngitis

Acute pharyngitis, an acute inflammation of he pharyngeal mucous membrane and the submucous lymphoid tissues, occurs mostly in winter and spring. According to modern medicine, the most common causes are bacterial or viral infection and rarely it is due to inhalation of irritant gases or ingestion of irritant lights. Clinically, it has the following main characteristics: dryness and soreness as well as a sensation of burning in the throat. In traditional Chinese medicine it belongs to the categories of "Hóu bì" (inflammation of the throat) or "Hóu fēng" (acute throat trouble).

ETIOLOGY AND PATHOGENESIS

Due to abnormal climate, unseasonable weather and carelessness about daily life, defense mechanism of the lung becomes so instable that the wind-heat evil takes advantage to attack the throat through the mouth and nose, causing damage of the lung and pathogenic heat to flare up with the result of swelling and pain of the throat. In this way, the disease occurs.

MAIN SYMPTOMS AND SIGNS

1. Pain of the throat, which becomes more severe when swallowing dryly.
2. Fever of 37.5℃ - 39℃, general discomfort, headache, poor appetite and constipation.
3. Diffuse congestion and swelling in the pharynx, particularly in the faux, edema of cion, possible coating on the posterior pharyngeal mucous wall and tonsils with secretion, in most cases, enlargement and tenderness of lymph nodes in the neck.
4. Red, tender tongue with thin, whitish or light yellowish fur, and floating and rapid pulse.

MAIN POINTS OF DIAGNOSIS

1. Dryness, a sensation of burning heat and soreness of the throat are present. When the patient swallows without food, the soreness becomes more severe. Or there may be itching and cough.
2. The patient runs a fever, the temperature ranging in most cases from 37.5℃ - 39℃. The accompanying symptoms of all-over discomfort, headache and nausea may occur.

3. The retropharynx mucous membranes congest diffusively, swell and become bright red. The lymph follicles are red and swollen, with exudates on the retropharynx wall. The lateral pharyngeal bands also show redness and swell. The lymph nodes may be enlarged and have tenderness.

4. The white blood count often increases.

Chronic pharyngitis, a chronic inflammation o the pharyngeal mucous membrane and submucous lymphoid tissues, is often caused by unthorough – going treatment of acute pharyngitis or repeated occurrences of upper respiratory tract infection and it is related to high – dust environment. Clinically it manifests itself as itching, dryness, soreness of the throat, cough, a feeling of foreign body or obstruction in the throat. It belongs to the category of "Hóu bi" in traditional Chinese medicine.

ETIOLOGY AND PATHOGENESIS

1. sore throat due to yin deficiency

There is general *yin* deficiency in the lung and kidney, or *yin* deficiency of the lung and kidney due to repeated occurrences of pharyngitis by wind and heat, or due to injury of *yin* caused by febrile diseases. With *yin* deficiency in he lung, body fluid is too insufficient to nourish the throat and with *yin* deficiency of the kidney and hyperactivity of fire due to *yin* deficiency, asthenic fire ascends to the throat, resulting in blockage of pharyngeal channels, disorder of qi and flaring-up of asthenic fever. In this way, the disease occurs.

2. sore throat due to yang deficiency

There is general *yang* deficiency, or impairment of *yang-qi* due to improper treatment of prolonged illness, or deficient *yin* affecting *yang* due to excessive sexual life, which leads to insufficiency of *yang-qi* and floating of asthenic *yang* up to the throat. In this way, the disease occurs.

MAIN SYMPTOMS AND SIGNS

1. Sensations of a foreign body, itching, burning, dryness and slight pain in the pharynx.

2. Dark reddish congestion of mucous membrane o the pharynx and slight edema of cion.

MAIN POINTS OF DIAGNOSIS

1. The patient has discomfort, dryness and itching, swelling and soreness, a feeling of foreign body in the throat or being stuck with sputum. He or she often wants to make a slight cough or irritated cough.

2. The patient has a sensation of obstruction and fullness in the throat and a feeling of being blocked when swal-

lowing without any food but no difficulty in eating.

3. The patient is apt to feel nausea and vomiting when he or she gets up in the morning.

4. Examination shows that the mucous membrane of the retropharyngeal wall becomes dark red and congestive, or there are dilatation of micrangium, attachment of exudates, hyperplasia of lymphoid follicles, red swelling and thickening of the lateral pharyngeal bands and pachynsis of the uvula.

Recipe 1
Ingredients
 wild chrysanthemum flower（*Flos Chrysanthemi*）
            12 g
 ophiopogon root（*Radix Ophiopogonis*） 12 g
 honeysuckle flower（*Flos Lonicerae*） 12 g
Process Infuse all them with boiling water.
Directions Take it as drink.
Indications Pharyngitis.

Recipe 2
Ingredients
 honeysuckle flower（*Flos Lonicerae*） 9 g
 scrophularia root（*Radix Scrophulariae*） 9 g
 Chinese white olive（*Fructus Canarii*） 9 g
Process Decoct them in right amount of water, sift out the decoction from dregs.

Directions　Take it as drink, one dose daily.
Indications　Pharyngitis.

Recipe 3
Ingredients
　　peppermint (*Herba Menthae*)　　　　5 g
　　green tea (*Folium Cameliae Viride*)　　5 g
　　borneol (*Borneolum*)　　　　　　　0.2 g
Process　Infuse all them with boiling water for 3 minutes.
Directions　Take it as drink.
Indications　Pharyngitis.

Recipe 4
Ingredients
　　fresh lophatherum (*Herba Lophatheri*)
　　　　　　　　　　　　　　　　　　10 – 15 g
　　ophiopogon root (*Radix Ophiopogonis*)　6 g
　　green tea (*Folium Cameliae Viride*)　　1 g
Process　Cut the first two ingredients into pieces, infuse them and tea in boiling water for 10 minutes.
Directions　Take it as drink.
Indications　Pharyngitis.

Recipe 5
Ingredients

honeysuckle flower (*Flos Lonicerae*)   9 g
forsythia fruit (*Fructus Forsythiae*)   9 g
boat - fruited sterculia   6
crystal sugar   right amount

Process   Decoct the honeysuckle flower and forsythia fruit in 300 ml of water in a pot, when the 200 ml of decoction left, then add in the and seal the container for 30 minutes, then season it with crystal sugar.

Directions   Take it warmly one dose daily for several days.

Indications   Pharyngitis.

Recipe 6

Ingredients

scrophularia root (*Radix Scrophulariae*) 15 g
ophiopogon root (*Radix Ophiopogonis*)   9 g
liquorice (*Radix Glycyrrhizae*)   3 g

Process   Decoct them in right amount of water.
Directions   Take it as drink, one dose daily.
Indications   Pharyngitis.

SECTION 10 Toothache

Recipe 1
Ingredients
    mulberry leaf（*Folium Mori*）   10 g
    chrysanthemum flower（*Flos Chrysanthemi*）   10 g
    crystal sugar   right amount
Process Decoct them in right amount of water.
Directions Take it as drink, one dose daily.
Indications Toothache.

Recipe 2
Ingredients
    glehnia root（*Radix Glehniae*）   30 g
    egg   2
    crystal sugar   right amount
Process Decoct glehnia root and eggs in right amount of water, when the eggs are well done, remove the shells of eggs, then go on decocting them

for 30 minutes, and season it with sugar.

Directions　Eat the eggs and drink the soup, one dose daily.

Indications　Toothache.

Recipe 3

Ingredients

　　honeysuckle flower (*Flos Lonicerae*)
　　　　　　　　　　　　　　　　30 g
　　chrysanthemum flower (*Flos Chrysanthemi*)　　　　　30 g
　　white sugar　　　　　right amount

Process　Decoct the honeysuckle flower and chrysanthemum in boiling water for 5 minutes.

Directions　Take it as drink, one dose daily.

Indications　Toothache.

Recipe 4

Ingredients

　　fragrant solomonseal rhizome (*Rhizoma Polygonati Odorati*)　　　　15 g
　　eclipta (*Herba Ecloptae*)　　9 g
　　vinegar　　　　　right amount

Process　Decoct the fragrant solomonseal rhizome and eclipta in right amount of water, add in the vinegar.

Directions　Take it one dose daily for 3 to 5 days successively.

Indications　Toothache.

Recipe 5

Ingredients

　　black soybean (*Semen Sojae Nigrum*)
　　　　　　　　　　　　　　right amount
　　millet wine　　　　　　right amount

Process　Decoct the black soybean in right amount of millet wine until it is well done.

Directions　gargle with the decoction.

Indications　Toothache.

Chapter Six

SECTION 11 Acute Tonsillitis

Acute tonsillitis is an acute nonspecific inflammation of the palatal tonsillae. Its clinical features are fever, headache, sore throat which is aggravated when swallowing, and reddened and swollen palatal tonsillae. It is called "Fēng rè rǔ é" or "é fēng", both referring to acute tonsillitis caused by pathogenic wind-heat.

ETIOLOGY AND PATHOGENESIS

It is related to pathogenic wind and heat which invade through the mouth and nose to attack the lung and stomach, resulting in the condition that heat in the lung ascends and attacks the throat by the lung meridian; or related to accumulation of heat in the stomach and spleen due to preference for spicy and greasy food and further attack of pathogenic wind and heat, resulting in accumulated heat in the throat.

MAIN SYMPTOMS AND SIGNS

1. Fever around 40℃.
2. Sore throat aggravated by swallow, even difficulty in swallow, pain radiating to the ear.
3. Redness and swelling in tonsil, purulent secretion in the opening of crypt, congestion in pharyngeal mucosa, submaxillary lymphadenovarix with tenderness.

MAIN POINTS OF DIAGNOSIS

1. The patient shivers with fever (the highest temperature may be around 40℃) and has accompanying headache and soreness o the limbs. In infant patient convulsion may present.
2. Sore throat occurs and it may radiate to the ears. The pain becomes more severe when the patient swallows and there is even dysphagia in severe cases.
3. The palatal tonsils congest and swell or there may be yellow - white exudate on the lacunae, which in severe cases forms a false membrane that can be easily erased.
4. There may be congestion of the throat as well as redness and swelling of or small white dots on the retropharyngeal lymph follicles.
5. There may be swelling and tenderness of the lymph

nodes in the angle of mandible.

6. There is an increase in the number of the white blood cells and neutrophils.

7. The onset is abrupt and its duration is short. Generally it can get cured in 5 – 7 days.

Recipe 1

Ingredients

    honeysuckle flower (*Flos Lonicerae*)   15 g
    reed Rhizome (*Rhizoma Phragmitis*)   15 g
    scrophularia root (*Radix Scrophulariae*) 12 g
    belamcanda rhizome (*Rhizoma Belamcandae*)
                                                    12 g

    subprostrate sophora root (*Radix Sophorae Subprostrate*)   12 g
    isatis root (*Radix Isatidis*)   12 g
    Radix Scutellariae   12 g
    forsythia fruit (*Fructus Forsythiae*)   12 g
    arctium fruit (*Fructus Arctii*)   10 g
    peppermint (*Herba Menthae*)   10 g

Process   Decoct them in right amount of water to get 350 – 400 ml of decoction.

Directions   Take the decoction twice daily.

Indications   Tonsillitis.

Recipe 2

Dermatoses

Ingredients

black edible fungus（*Auricularia*） 10 g

Process Bake the black edible fungus dry and grind it into fine powder.

Directions Blow it to the affected part, once daily.

Indications Tonsillitis.

Recipe 3

Ingredients

acid plum	10 g
olive	50 g
white sugar	right amount

Process Soak the wild plum and olive in right amount of water in an earthenware pot over one day, then decoct it over a slow fire. Season it with sugar.

Directions Take the decoction once daily.

Indications Tonsillitis.